FRAGS

FRAGS

by
Page Nelson

Another Sparrow Press

© Copyright 2018 Page Nelson

Frags is a textual object fully and exclusively belonging to the Page Nelson Charitable Trust, its successors, assigns, legatees, devisees, and mortmainders and is protected by copyright and its equivalent in the following countries and areas, as authorized: United States (Title 17, US Code), Canada, (the Copyright Act of Canada), Europe (the European Convention on Copyright, EUROCONCAT), and in all other countries (Copyright Law of the People's Republic of China, as amended in the Decision of February 26, 2010, by the Standing Committee of the National People's Congress on Amending the Copyright Law of the PRC). Any use, reuse, analogue or digital transmission, replication or republication, in whole or in part, including duplication of individual words, not exempting "a", "an", "the" and "is", is strictly prohibited and will result in penalties civil and/or criminal. For permissions, directives and dying declarations, contact the Trust. The author's assertion of his moral right not to be identified as the author of the cited work may result in disablement but not forfeiture of some or all of the aforesaid reservations and rights, as modified *quantum meruit.*

ISBN: 978-1-941066-29-4
Cataloging-at-Publication data
Nelson, Page, 1952-
Frags / by Page Nelson.
 1. Aphorisms and apothegms.
 II. Title.   2017. RDA-NEG8
PN6271. N442 2018   CAP/NOTCIP

Catalogued to pre-2014 conventions in conformity with standards approved by the American Association of Cataloging Rules Conservation (AACRC).

Cover photography by Guy Mantis
(Mantis Galleries, New York)

Book design by Jo-Anne Rosen
(Petaluma, California)

Die alten, bösen Lieder,
Die Träume bös bos' und arg,
Die last uns jetzt begraben,
Holt einen grossen Sarg.

Wisst ihr warum der Sarg wohl
So gross und schwer mag sein?
Ich senkt' such meine Liebe
Und meinen Schmerz hinein!

Heinrich Heine (in the musical setting by Schumann)

What follows is an introduction of no importance. This latest work proves my prior volume, too significantly entitled *Vacating the Premises*, to have been an objective falsehood or at least a fiction when it announced itself "the last of my experiments in aphoristical exposition." If *Frags* resembles my earlier titles in form and content, it differs in tone, being sharper and duller. If these precedent works were truly fragmentary, that is, hypothetically assimilable into an aesthetic whole, *Frags* asserts no such restorative potential, its propositions either *splinters simpliciter* or pedestrian declamations, the one too jagged, the other too amorphous for any restorative unification, a collection not of fragments but of something even more particulate. Such disjunctions of focus are typical of artists late in their creative careers. Joyce after *Ulysses*, James after *The Golden Bowl*, and even Shakespeare in his "romances" are likewise producers of "out of form" works that evidence their character as after-the-fact effects, instances, for all their accomplishment and interest (if so), of aesthetic beta-decay.

No matter. *One's relation to art is relational.* Like our meeting with persons, some involvements are significant, others aren't, with predictions of value or effect, dubious and nearly always overvalued. (This world of 2018 would be but very minutely changed had Joyce died in 1910 (before *Ulysses*).[1] Yet in every life

---

[1] One loss would be Joyce's word "quark", adopted by Gell-Mann to designate an important atomic particle. My alternative term, "blippy" or "blip" has not yet acquired general acceptance.

some random encounter may and usually does change that life (the collective field of these alterations being a society). So, my advice to any by-chance-acquired appreciators (in or about the year 2050) would be, firstly, to read my novel *A Book of Emblems* (available from Amazon and fine books shop everywhere) to understand the contextual background of these philosophical forays. Secondly, to not accept my interpretation of any event, person, or object, nor endorse anyone else's, including you own, without strenuous scrutiny and repletive re-examination. Thirdly, do not assume you know what I am feeling, for example, paragraph 121 seems bitter but only if you are missing slap stick comedy so obvious it is self-obscuring or are unaware of the almost Derridean subterfuging effects (or defects) occurring before a continuously receding personal horizon along which are many more x's of problem/solution than intersecting y's (whys) of inquiry, in other words, a *cantus firmus* that is fundamentally a fermata. Fifthly and lastly, pardon my didactic, declamatory tone, portending an antic disposition and preferred style that is baroque and broken.

Among my tenebrous themes (darkening many lighter ones) are: sexual betrayal, which offends one's natural instincts, lying, which undermines one's subjective ideation, and death which menaces one's existential totality. Without devaluing these experiences natural, personal, and existential, they are best taxonomized not as habitations but as way stations to be traversed to an integrated and more compassionate being.

This said, the book seeks no readers, its expressive condition that of a man sitting alone and talking to himself which if it cannot guarantee total truthfulness (what could?) does facilitate complete candor. As to why I would further bother to publish such a transcript (legally classified as a "dying declaration"), I can only explain by way of analogy. Nineteenth century armies did not lack for flag bearers even though the position was known to be terminal. Men volunteered for a variety of known and unknow reasons: pride, dutifulness, a desire to prove themselves, a death wish. But in order for the sacrifice to exist in this form, there had to be a flag. For my purposes, a draft journal left in desk drawer to be trashed upon my demise does not satisfy my requirements of negative action, a black flag furled, the way twenty or thirty copies, a few of them dust gathering in a libraries or bookshops, does. As to why this is, I am reminded of a law case from a few decades ago which much impressed me. My mind is shy about locking up the details but the main facts were as follows.[2] An old Jewish lawyer had decided to litigate *pro se* a civil action that everyone knew, on legal if not moral grounds, was a losing one. Since he himself recognized his advocacy was hopeless, he was asked why he still presented the case. His eloquent response, more subtle than I can relate, was

---

2   Subsequent to the above writing, I have learned a partial transcript of the trial is recorded in MOV.IV.4.1-398.

that temperament drives action and his temper was to pursue a losing action rather than do nothing. His final words to the reporter were, like a last stand of flags, "Are you answered?"

Charlottesville, Sept. 2017-Aug. 2018

(To those who find this preface stylistically infelicitous, I can only reply that it reads better in Chinese and German and that I thank, in advance, my translators (Vielen Dank and Gan Xiel) into those languages.)

A Note on Form

The vertebrae of the work consist of short, aphoristic expositions (presented in order of composition) in the Germanic tradition of brief mediation rather than a constitutively witty remark. Ten of the statements are followed by poems (from my previously published volumes) when it was perceived the old poem augmented a new meaning. For alternative reading, an anonymous bibliofile (sic) has contributed snippet reviews (marked RR, for "recommended reading") of some of the best books published in 2017. Additionally, in the interest of textual dimensionality, there are two extended insertions of "fragmentary fiction" or "frag-fic."[3] Parenthetical statements function, as usual, as supplemental observations. Bracketed statements, appearing in the differing type face Garamond, are oppositional or dismissive. Both commentaries are "asides" intended to shape a literary form consonant with my belief that truth, such as it is, is not a position or pronouncement but a process and dialogue, a dialectical working

---

[3] *Fragmentary Fiction* and *Frag-fic* are copy-righted and patent pending phrases and practices belonging to Page Nelson. Any use, re-use or abuse without the express permission of Page Nelson, his successors, assigns, legatees, devisees, and mortmainderees is prohibited. Violators are subject to civil or criminal penalties, or both. For permissions and all inquiries, write; "Dagwood, Digby and Dogbolt (LLC), Solicitors and Guarantors for/of the Assigns, Legatees, Devisees and Mort-Manatees of The Page Nelson Charitable Trust, 1641 Rugby Avenue, Charlottesville, Virginia 22903, USA."

out not of "truth and consequences" but "truth and circumstances."

[Sounds more like "Pomposity and Circumstances" to me.]

(Hopefully, the book is unreadable.)

By way of introduction. On rereading KM's mosaical notebooks, one's complacencies (and comforts) are constantly tugged at by her fragile pride, demeaning tactical lies and daily lived intensities – the bright fluoresce of desperation, the haunted look of a doomed Japanese doll who has read her death warrant and noted the open date.[4] She is often short of funds and never well. You want to time travel and infuse her with cash and whatever we treat TB with.

Consonant with the grain of time, only she can do the giving, bequeathing to us: completed stores, sketches for stories, household accounts, notes on her reading and medical appointments, routine diary entries, memoirs of her family and amours, recordations of hope and despair, lots of so-so poems – facets of a life that looks shabby and was definitely short. Yet she had an uncanny appreciation of beauty, loved and to some extent was loved, achieving in her art a handful of exquisite, gem-like narratives. And in her person, what? A pale violet, briefly flowering.

[God, I detest sentimental, heart on sleeve writing like this but at least we're forewarned of the emulatingly disorganized mass of "not much" to follow and of our weedy author's self-conceit as a common flower of ordinary beauty – a buttercup, a dandelion, a corn(y) flower. As to his latest idol along "Dark Lady" lines, she

---

4   *The Notebooks of Katherine Mansfield*, University of Minnesota Press, 2002.

was a liar and a manipulator of the most unrecoverable kind, more stinging nettle than blaue Blume.]

(A liar who separated herself from truth the more to adore it.)

Such a book, while having an organizing principal, in this instance, a generally chronological presentation of her papers, lacks a determining artistic structure. It may be skimmed, skipped, scanned progressively or retrogressively, perused in sequence as a kind of history or dipped into for poetic epiphanies, a text where every individual reading is random, not regulated. My aim: the presentation not of an assemblage or assortment but of a particulate unity that treelike can be perceived distinctly and holistically from any point of the compass, close-in and at distance.[5]

[Amen and Amen!]

---

5   Recommended dosage is one or two encapsulations, taken in the evening with wine (5 oz.), beer (12 oz). or cannabis (500 mg.), not exceeding sixteen units weekly.

1   It was the best kind of American parade, barely organized, by all appearances, *ad hoc*. In stately procession were six or seven gleaming antique cars followed by clumps of children, high school bands quietly bearing instruments like soldiers at ease and a festive colophon of fire trucks. It was hard to say what was best, the ballet school, adequate marchers even as they made swans rising with their hands or the two tired men carrying the 4 H Club of Albemarle banner, limping green and gold, behind which walked a boy with a bright-eyed rooster.

2   It seems the trees have conspired, all the leaves dropping in the night.

3   The righteous demand the Lee equestrian statue be pulled down and haven't the imagination or magnanimity to let his mount remain, memorial to horses in war.

[Yes, a judicious use of acetylene would have resolved the whole issue. But never underestimate the rigidity of the morally upright.]

4   He appreciated the symmetry – as he'd had no choice in the day of his conception, he'd have none in his demise.

5   As a strategist of lies, he was excellent, only giving utterance to those he could tactically believe in. {NAM}[6] |cf. no.50|

6   *Battleship Yamoto.* Jan Morris writes (2018) "She was beautiful." Yes and No. In her nautical prime, the ship was imposing, powerful. And in the brief hour of her destruction, catastrophically compelling. Beauty only comes in with the infusion of time, a grasping of the entire sequence, keel laying to death knell, a perceived added dimension of temporality and tragic transition. Not only objects are rendered beautiful in this *ideal* way but sometimes too the rare individual. (Marie Antoinette.)

7   One almost chuckles, what were those Germans and Japs thinking with their Bismarcks and Yamotos that for all their complex lethality were basically big buckets begging to be punctured and sunk, an awareness that hasn't stopped us from building floating mammoths that are twice as long, weighty and, as gigantism always is, *delicate.* It's the old, old story: before catharsis the diagnostic terms are "over confidence" and "lack of insight" – the sheer inability, as likewise about our lives, to credit the worst that can happen. After, one word serves. Fate.

---

6   Shorthand, a cipher signifying "Not about me."

8   He related to his thoughts the way any old dog does fleas – while there weren't as many of them as before, they still itched.

9   The young find the old imponderably pathetic – how had they gotten that way? The aged bitterly pity the young: why are there so many of them, callow and predictably clueless. If the young can play their trump card, beauty, and the old theirs, pride in endurance, it's a fact that beauty will not endure and that endurance isn't beautiful.

10   In every American city except the youth attracting trendy ones – Aspen, Austin, Palo Alto, the streets are congested with the obese. Americans, who were first even before the French to invent fat activists and advocates, really need a fat theorist to explain what it means. It is certainly expressive of something. Already established are the heavy-weight motorcyclist clubs, the Killer Carbs, the Lords of Lard, three hundred pounds per Harley, loud slabs of menace moving like a landslide.

RR: The Book of Annie by Blackie Collins. This is the story of Annie Oakley translated into a dystopian future when the earth has become a series of reefs and shoals where people have developed fins and war with dolphins for survival.

---

11   His instincts told him that Gillian Rose's book on Hegel was a good one, but at the end, he realized he didn't understand it, hadn't understood it in the middle or at the beginning either. It was time to put Hegel on the mantel and let him gather dust. He might just as well never have taken him down. The entire effort was a bust.[7]

12   "No time for Hegel or Kant." I've not only read this kind of remark but have heard it spoken. It boils downs to "No thought for thinking", which amounts to stupidity. It is tantamount to "No action for activity." which would be death. The final equating, that stupidly equals death, is of the type that readers of Kant and Hegel, in their "at midnight, all cows are back" prejudice are, perhaps, too inclined to.make.

["Not one person has been bettered (excepting professors) nor has the world been improved in any way, by the study of Kant and Hegel. It is not an instance of useless knowledge but of useless non-knowledge". "You

---

[7] Hegel's own palliating prescription for this condition is "Die hochste Reife und Stufe, die irgend etwas erreichen kann, ist diejenige, in welcher sein Untergang beginnt."

don't understand that K and H are synthesizing *critical* philosophers, whose positive influence on physics and evolutionary biology…" "Everything you've said on this subject is balderdash. How's that for a critical posture – and one without "benefit" of a single word from Kant or Hegel." "Except *critical*."]

13   Walking in the university library stacks, he was overwhelmed by the spectra of book spines, the medal ribbons of Thoth.

["Err, that won't work, Old Sport. It's a trope that was dead on arrival, lost on the way, abandoned on the doorstep. "Are you saying I must kill my beauties?" "Yes, even when they are and this isn't." "But what about Shakespeare's riffs – Richard in the dungeon, Ophelia taking a dip, does he kill his?" "No, Old Sport, but you're no Shakespeare." "Well, according to the Oxford editors, neither was he. He was a committee. And stop calling me "Old Sport."]

14   Reading Scott Fitzgerald, a sense of the degradation of our experience in exchanging ocean liners for planes. On ships, one could meditate relatively unwearied upon travel itself, the days of humanly featureless seas cleaning the mental palette for novelty. Now, we arrive fatigued from flight's tight seats and stale air, unprepared for perception, suffocated, still in the grip of old time zones and habits of seeing. Everywhere

looks the same. We've saved time and lost place.

Our argument turned into two vibratory machines that were elaborate solid, sounds, emanating our contestations, working them out, a gradual fitting into clinch. We left them in their conciliating space and exited unto the grand canals, the palazzi carved in enamel, set like teeth either side of the mineral green tongue.

15   My minor talent makes very little light but in a dim literary age, not for that to be sneezed at – and put out.

[Not for you to say, Old Sport. Ach-choo!]

16   The only cure for his narcissism was an injury distressful enough to discomfort living with himself so that if he would live, he'd have to turn towards others not from virtue or choice but from necessity. Since the remedy was effective only when it was painful, he had to be grateful the dose had been administered so generously.

['You say. But I can't imagine a piece of writing more self-centered than this." "Self-centered, not self-absorbed. I state an identity and describe the location and conditions of my landfall. It's a message in a bottle." "Message *out* of a bottle, more like. *Virginia Gentleman?*"[8] "Well. thank you, I hope I am."]

17   Some events so painful one can't live with them yet to turn away from them is to live inauthentically in a place of unreality. One claws out a space of accommodation, in touch with the horror but not enveloped by it, a place of high energy expenditure-maintenance which it if doesn't de-evolve into corrosive anxiety and distractiveness may yet be the launching pad for one's highest achievements. |cf.no.166|

[N's affirmative ending here seems forced or false, at any rate, unearned. He had no doubt viewed (televised) too many rocket launches as a 1960's child.]

18   In the daily parade of thoughts and images, one is too continuously painful to repeatedly encounter. So, you pluck it out and wall in it. Only now it's a room in the habitation of your life. You've closed the door but the handle always draws your hand.

---

8   Controversy flares as to whether this mildly antiseptic (and inflammable) fluid, which undergoes two preliminary distillations in in Frankfort KY before its third (and casking) in Virginia might be more appropriately branded as "Kentucky Swigger."

Still Life

A life of still lifes: domestic scenes,
pleasant rooms, plates of food,
trusted friends, their conversations,
nick-nacks, each meaningful, arranged.
Here are flowers from the garden,
placed in a vase. Between color
and scent there is an interchange,
a play like themes in a quartet.
This is my life, floor after floor of light.
At the root of it all, a black machine,
massive, thick walled, hot to the touch.
Through its little slit for in sight, look.
Flames, rage.

19   He was drawn to his shame (his own pain) like a moth to flame.

[Post-traumatic stress syndrome occurs when a life-threatening event takes up lodging in the mind as a free-floating memory; unanchored by the brain's usual retention centers, the event seems to be recurring continuously. The question in your case – whose life was threatened – yours, your inamorata's, her lover's? Knowing you, your reply would involve some trinitarian mystery where you suffer the hazards of all three, hanging like a proxy Odin from an ersatz ash tree. *Pathei mathos* and all that jazz.]

20   In the Edda manuscripts, Odin constantly warns "avoid treacherous people", presumably as public service. But he does it so frequently you suspect he's talking to himself, as if he knew he was an easy mark for any low key (Loki?) trickster. What's the point anyway? It is not as if the treacherous wear an identifying sign or indicate themselves by winking an eye or flicking the tongue so they can be avoided in advance of their actions. They look like everyone else; for all practical purposes, they are everyone else. Everyone except yourself. You've never betrayed anyone, have you? No one but yourself. And where do you go to escape yourself? The world, a place to bustle in.

21   Those writers who condemn the passive voice are like musicians who only compose in major keys. Yes, we get the message – they are as direct as they are superficial.

At the back of her teeth, we were tartars, sticking around for a while, then washed away by the floss of fluss – a process, they say, of decay. But hang on, turns out dental detritus is memorious, they can do a tiny core sample of its DNA and read the menu of everything you've ever chewed, so many chines of beef, porks of pig, bushels of broccoli, fork spins of spaghetti, it makes my headache, my teeth tingle to think of it, including every kiss, each beseeching – I'm not kidding and if you say "Hey I brush three times a day and get hygiened every six months" – it don't matter, Morphy – it's the salvia, it mineralizes, her least tongue-in-cheek communique engrained in four molecules of your best molar, and you can't even remember her name but that's okay, your unconscious is working it out, (don't even mention extraction – that hurts), tracking the trace – oh yeah, Tracey and this, as they say in maritime engineering terms, the oil flush flash to propel me from All Halt and Idle to All Ahead Amble. (Call it preamble.)

22   He mailed copies of his latest book to six distant friends and a year later, not one of them had said thanks or even acknowledged receipt. This was extremely gratifying. Now he knew the book was embarrassingly bad or so good that envy compelled silence. Naturally, he believed the latter.

[You don't need a degree in criticism to know that the book, like 95% of them, was so-so and thus ordinary, properly inciting no comment whatsoever.]

23   I suspect all that stuff about aboriginal peoples venerating the aged is hogwash. The young of the tribe learned that looking attentive seemed respectful and was the easiest way to ignore the elderly who,

half-dead and knowing they are repulsive, are happy to accept nodding respect.

24   Alcohol lowered his intellectual aspirations. His intelligence was entirely adequate at lesser altitudes, in thicker air.

25   He came to understand that the mistakes he'd made were not "on the edge of the knife" decisions in which the correct choice had been within reach. No, it was just a fact that he wasn't very bright and everything in his life had followed from that. *What a relief.*

26   When a woman makes a man a sap, the first question he needs to ask is "Was this a violation or a fulfillment?"

27   He was such a sap, she could have knocked him over the head with her falsehood, as in a sense she did, when, modestly smiling, she said "I've decided to do my dissertation on lies and liars" – and five years after came out with *"Lies and Liars in Greek Tragedy"* – and still he would have believed her. Later, much later, he reflected that given her facility in Greek and mendacity, they should have just awarded her an honorary degree – no need for her to spell it out. |cf.no.134|

27a Don't blame traitors; they are opportunistic predators, as innocent as sharks. Condemn the faithful, who wanting a wound, bleed a gush of trust.

28 While a few persons are brave all the time (the famous Lord Gort, for one) and a few always timid, most of us are courageous in certain situations and along certain lines. Our courage has its individual style. As a co-worker, I often witnessed our bosses trying to bully her out of her better ideas. Jobs, hers among them, were at stake. Her response was measured, almost lofty, serenely resistant. She didn't give an inch. It was a pretty thing to see and it caught my eye like the glint of a blade.

29 Pretty soon, according to the silicon tycoons, we'll be popping our daily immortality pill. And that's the end of serious art. It was facing death or more exactly, death behind us, pushing, that made us create – expression as desperation. (This overemphasizes the expressive element over the epistemic. Artists seek a deeper understanding of truth and beauty via the creation or replication of these qualities in their art. All art is, broadly considered, memetic, which explains the stagnant state of aesthetics, post-Plato.)

30   The bay of books was congested with 500-page dreadnaughts – time to deploy the light forces. (The general problem: the surplus (or superabundance) of art, (measured in annual million tons), that effects, like a surfeit response, its own indigestibility. What matters is the meaning-making ritual of processing: massive amounts of junk money (money many generations derived from products, services or labor; money made by money a hundred derivatives ago) is exchanged for massive amounts of junk art and the objects then stored away in collectors' cellars, bank vaults, valuables' warehouses, museums, or circulated, in slow relays, back to galleries and studio annexes. The stuff can only be exhibited in small quantities or the invented/invested value collapses. Everyone understands this.)

31   In time, he acquired a "smiling public man" manner, a snakeskin like *asp*ect that didn't become him despite his being naturally forked tongued. {NAM}

RR: The Welcome Guest by Ann Bachtic. In this collection of stories, the stark aggregates of ageing, friends reuniting, loneliness and lawn care are common threads.

---

32   The greatest threat to humanity isn't a pandemic, stray meteor or nuclear war. It's AI. In fifty years, we will have given sway to quantum computers of immense power and autonomy, able to manufacture and manage an army of robots to maintain and defend their sustaining environment. Humanity will just be fuzz on the orange or dust on the apple. Something that with no evil intent, you, they, just blow away. Meantime, it's old style ironic, seeing the successes of Silicon Valley securing for their children and grandchildren not the promised paradise but a future of (at best) grand futility. |cf.no.96|

Art historian junior grade (grad student), one cool triptych – a non-virgin Mary – she looked best in blue, flanked (ha-ha?) by the Saints Cunnilingus and Fellatio (of Priapus.) Busy with her studies and working part time as an editorial assistant on Harvard's edition of John Ruskin, called familiarly "the Crimson Ruskin" and referred to by intimates as "the Red Rug" (red being the binding) and "rug", rather than Rus because this posh carpet, unrolled at the length of two vols annually, would smother any subsequent edition for a hundred years … furnish a room.

33   It shouldn't be viewed too pathetically, the desolation of wine bottles empty except for the clarified

light, the labels still flirting but futilely, no body to back them, nothing left of last night's bush except a rim of red dregs.

[The above contains Fine Writing. Readers sensitive to Fine Writing may experience vertigo, upset ecstatics, rapid heartbeat and hot flashes. For relief, cold compasses or pabulum of print such as *The Wall Street Journal*, *Reader's Digest* or *The New York Times* (Business Section) should be applied to the eyes. If reactive symptoms do not improve within twelve hours, consult your local aesthetician.]

In the stemmed glass's refraction,
he reflected on his life and work,
the still lives -- quintets, quartets,
now trios of bottles.
In a few decades, if he lived,
he'd reach pure deduction,
only a canvas stretched and primed,
a thin ground of color.
Then he'd close the door on perfection,
on the studio's vacant easels and frames,
the wine bottles in their dress of labels
and copes of dust, solo or in clusters,
like guests at the exhibition
suddenly hushed.

34   The fire was out. But if the wood had been good, the ashes would sweeten the soil in the spring.

RR. Fire from the dragon. Edited by Adm Stelle Blair. Insider accounts of the Sino-American naval war. Pushed back to the Guam-Australian line, US forces stand firm. What both sides are doing in preparation for round two! (War Book Club selection. Made in USA.)

---

35   Pretty soon every "first world" home will have cute robots which will replace pets, being smarter, cleaner and able to anything you ask them except love you. But people will imagine they are loved and usually that is good enough.

36   It was after he was decidedly disillusioned with her that he divined she had many admirable qualities only they were not the ones that had drawn him to her. (She was, for instance, very stinting of praise, an ungenerosity compounded of insecurity and an incorruptible integrity in matters of intellect. On the bright side, if her holding back didn't incite him to his best efforts, what would?)[9]

---

[9] Lovers sit down to their prepared table for two, set already with two carafes labeled "Being Disappointed" and "Being Deceived" (mix them at risk). These are mere bitters, aperitifs to a stronger distilment, "Deeper knowledge, deeper love". But for that, they must stay at the table and wait.

37   He walked around saying "I'm a tragic figure" and he actually was except for his broadcasting the self-identification which revealed him to be, more exactly, an idiot. {NAM}

38   Samuel Butler (in his notebooks), second rate in a small-scale way; Spengler, second rate in a vast way. The temptation is to be witty and quip that the former is superior to the latter. Bur since Spengler's ponderosa does occasionally rope in the stray steer of an idea, one needed to resist it.

39   A tight island, smug with grievance. Not a description of actual Ireland, only of a type she might have become and was in episodes: an IRA captain asking some guy to recite the rosary (as a test) while calmly preparing to gouge out his eyes.

40   He hadn't lived past his defeats the way he had his victories. They still seethed volcanically and it cheered him immensely to stoke the flames.

41   The entertainment industry spends billions of dollars designing and developing zombies, vampires, killer aliens and revived dinosaurs to terrify when really, any clock face with a second hand should suffice.

Now you are wondering – exactly how did such an academic mammoth land on these our culturally impoverished shores when everybody knows every bit of Ruskin's journals, manuscripts, proofs, and foul papers reside in the Britannic Isles (except, very conveniently and insignificantly, a small ream of papers gathered by that collector of wide taste but narrow means, Henry Cabot-Cod, and donated to Houghton). Well, it took what it always does: a man or woman with a plan. Our man: Marty Bronstein, who after getting tenure on the back of his bulked-up dissertation (*Rossetti and the Radicals*) was, between sets of sweaty tennis at the Faculty Club (gym), looking for a new venture and happened on Ruskin … it was a bee in his bonnet, a bug in his bung, a poke in his pocket. For wasn't "Rusty" undergoing yet another of his revivals? Didn't people say he was the precursor of Deleuze, a multicultural syncretist centuries ahead of his time?

42   She had, deservedly, a good opinion of herself allied with and a very exact idea of the degree to which she should be admired. Too much was as disagreeable as too little. Well, he knew he's never get that right and so one day he just pitched right in –"I love you."

[I can imagine her response.]

43   Suddenly, her kisses tasted differently.

[Is that all? Do tell.]

44   After many tempests, we arrived in safe harborage just as dusk was falling and the lights were coming on along the piers.

RR: The Aphorist. By Bruno Hob. Bum poet Bradley Smith writes a volume of trite aphorisms as a joke only for it to become a best seller. A nation-wide book tour propels him to the depths of despair and sexual excess until he encounters redemption in the person of Coloradoan cow girl Jody Collins. (Rev. ed.)

---

45   It seemed to have been a happy house, retaining the dust of old summers (Manuscript variant: "the lusts of old summers", "dusts of old lusts.") |cf. no.174|

46   Since no one particularly pitied his wounds, he didn't anyone else's. He learned, as apparently everyone had, pity is an abstraction, not an action.

Marty knew the last attempt at a complete collation had been the Gentleman's Club Edition (Duckworth and Drake, London 1920) edited by Sir Lesley Stephen-Stephen, on his final pins, and Charles Tansley, Esq. Marty knew too that its every on-shelf instantiation was dissolving into a moraine of leather rot and paper flakes. Of course, Marty would need the imprimatur of the National Editors' Board (N.E.B), eight old nit-picking windbags who wrinkled their brows at all the source papers being overseas. But as Marty explained, he'd microfilm everything (image scanners a decade away), either done inhouse or licensed out. The files would be printed out stateside on paper (not even prisoners would work more than three hours at a microfilm reader – this had been tried on the Hoosier Whitcomb Riley, an edition congested with pent-up obscenities).[10] The big nibs (pens of brass) might still have baulked but Marty had been one of them's best boy in grad school and they relished the American acquisition of Ruskin like Grant took Richmond – by iron will, material advantage, and adequate management skills.

---

10   Notoriously, Riley's most famous poem appears as "The Old Qwimmin' Hole."

47   After a lifetime reaching for refinement, he ended up on the cusp of nothingness. Because nothing is purer than nothing.

48   How generous the unfaithful partner has been! How grateful the faithful should be, never having to worry about *that* again.

(Baudrillard says the shock of a trusted lover's infidelity can be so severe, one realizes the actuality of evil and, for relief, arrives at belief in God. I trust this is one of his Gallic jests. The enduring effects upon the faithful partner are self-pity and resentment, an undermining gyre of self-contempt.)

[No, the worst thing is that tenderness and generosity are unmasked as handmaidens to treachery. And so, weeping and wringing their hands, they are led to the wall and shot.]

49   A green tree teeming with small orange monkeys. Nature as artist. He had to chuckle with admiration. It wasn't, as design, at all obvious.

50   There he was, neatly dressed in a camel's hair sport coat (draped over his collapsing shoulders), Greek fisherman's hat (indoor wear), and new blue jeans, hectoring me on Cezanne in a thin, reedy voice, pausing

to chew on breath mints, his face so pale you felt you could almost see the bones and did the snaking blue veins. Green eyed, thin lipped, with wisps of blond hair – he looked like somebody's attempt at Lucifer – an awkward initial model but headed in the right direction – the composition lacking as yet two van Eyke angels on the wings, descending in jeweled, brocaded gowns, to whip some courtesy into him. |cf. no.5|

Auld Lang Syne

My thoughts found their enabling friend –
this new computer's search engine. It reeled you in.
Idling at work, (which I rarely do), I tapped a
   vectoring word or two
and there you were, in glowing pixels, courtesy
   of your institution –
A no-name private high school – not even a two-
   year college.
Guess I beat you in careering (Or did I? University
   librarian.)
You're instantly recognizable – but grown so
   very bald?
with great bags under your eyes and no the hint
   of grin.
You look pretty grim. What might be the cause?
Disappointing children, an unwise wife or wives?
It makes me sad, this widening time of separation

when once your thoughts (I thought) were nearer
   to me
than my own, why, we shared everything, cars,
   money,
nothing between such pals. What could break
   such bonds?
It's a tease to say I don't recall. It was that girl
who sends me a card every other year. She has
   no news
of you unless she's playing false again with me,
   with you.
(Wouldn't you agree – I was always true?)
It all comes back ... well, I'm tempted to mouse
   your page's
"please contact" or even pick up the phone –
   your voice!
Touching reconciliation. But on second thought,
   my first
before I began this search, given all I know of you,
I think not. You were my best friend, but friend,
   what a jerk!
(Floating above you on my screen, a thin grey
   reflection.
Books stacking up. Get back to work.)

50a   He could only be at peace with himself when he had enemies and happily (for him), he had no trouble making them. {NAM}

51   Irony can only be viable in an environment of meanings; it plays off one meaning and flirts with another. In our world of vast and uniform information, it has no purchase or purpose, a chess piece in a game of Go. What's left, the last holdout of old fashioned humanism: humor of an especially facetious and redoubtful kind.[11]

[This may strike unbiased readers as unpleasantly self-serving.]

52   His humor was like one of those wind-up toys, say a monkey with a drum, that pacing its mechanical track isn't funny until it stops, topples over and one's laughter can be taken to refer to the entire course.

53   Reading *The British Almananck*, 1821. A strange vibrant world of wooden ships, buildings no taller than six stories, horse conveyances, elaborate clothes, complicated codes of behavior and morality, populated by osiers, half-pay captains, quack doctors. "ladies of fashion", printer-republicans and far too many hanging judges. Try as I might, I cannot comprehend where this world went but sense it is where I'm headed

---

11   "Given recent history, art can no more be completely serious than it can be lighthearted. It is doubtful it was ever as serious as culture tried to convince us it was." Adorno, *Notes to Literature* 2. 253 (1991).

54   Resentment: a snake that no matter how many times you step on it, keeps biting back.

55   No man is an island but lots of them are swamps.

56   The elderly: children who think they know they secrets.

57   Flattery, like money, opens all doors and is a lot cheaper.

[These are the kind of too neat and facile "aphoristic type expressions" N. ostensibly despised, included in this collection, one supposes, as a provocation.]

58   While a wider existential orbit (more experiences, thoughts, friends) is better than a small one, the crucial question is "Can you ever *escape* your orbit?' That's where the interest lies.

So Ruskin's corpus would be new robed in unbendable boards tautly tarped in fore square crimson clothe of Flemish weave most luminous and durable, ANSI certified acid-free 1.2 mil paper to bear the press of newly founted 12 point Baskerville-Bonnet, to convey (or convoy), like superfluous gifts of the magi (frankincense? myrrh?), introductions general, historical and editorial, the vetted, denominated text, with notes, variable variants, a chronology, indices topical, personal and tropio-hermeneutical and, oh, an Acknowledgements section as long as a poet's novel. Go Bronstein! He'd secure (and keep) the grants, contact the holding intuitions, write the annual report, show the flag at conferences and hire the associate editor and editorial assistants who'd confirm the printout, determine/correct the copy text, proofreading it (three times!), (assisted by a supervisor at the press and a half-time accountant seconded from the athletic dept to pay the bills) and do all the crap work, which is to say the real work.

59   What was male circumcision but a crazy fad, a fetish practiced in mass by American physicians for no good medical reason so that between 1940 and 2010 they must have scalped a mountain of foreskins higher than Pike's Peak. Was it an artistic impulse, the satisfaction of rendering penises as baldheaded little men? If this discourse makes one physically uncomfortable (it gives me an ache in my crotch), keep in mind that at the level of organic truth, all of us are butchers' bits not yet chopped.

60   However large and closely placed the loud, cellulated hotels, the lively strip of boardwalk, the bathers shouting and bouncing in the surf, it all has a flickering, pointillistic aspect of temporality (it could disappear tonight or in a second) set beside the vast featureless sea, as does my life situated at the edge of another immensity.

61   The question where we might be after death (aside from the grave) can be answered with another question "Where were we before we were born?" If the reply was made, "Well, nowhere but we weren't created then" let's remember that anything created is subject to destruction. Against the improbability of any afterlife, might be waged the improbable odds that we had a life at all.

[Such questions are meaningless especially if probabilities are invoked. What is the probability of the universe existing? 100% you'd think but likely it was a lot less.]

62   I'm in sympathy with the Greenlander converts to Christianity who lost interest in it when they learned there were no seals in heaven. What kind of paradise separates us enterally from the things we love?

[So, you'd refuse paradise on the basis of no books, beer, or babes?]

63   Just as Buddhists mediate on the after-death decay of their bodies in the interest of truth, one should contemplate ugly betrayal by the loved one. While death is certain and the incidence of infidelity (in western countries) only about 25% for long term partners, this "preparatory mediation" is like insurance – if you need it, you really need it.

64   You'd think the highest point on earth would have been protected, preserved as a park. Instead, its unique status (like high human beauty) has attracted a host of attempters, with all the detritus of failure – shredded tents, littered oxygen canisters, and over 300 dead bodies frozen in place like steppingstones or signposts, too difficult at altitude to remove, the mountain turned into a charnel pile fulfilling the fate of its arbitrarily imposed colonial name –"ever rest".

NO FLOWERS

Time for the decennial botanic survey of Mt. Eyrie. So, the nearby university sent its graduate students upslope, in high summer, to the alpine and sub-alpine meadows to count the flowers.

What they found – not global warming's stratified supplanting of colder by warmer species but patchy die backs at all levels.

And when they tested the soils, deadly concentrations of potassium and calcium.

Then they noticed the groups of people, below summit, that held hands, bowed heads, one of them releasing into the uplift of wind, a pink grey plume.

Because Steve had climbed that peak, because Amy loved to hike, because grandma's eyes were blue as mountain sky. Because it was good to fulfill their final wishes, recycling the remains back to nature with no fuss, no flowers.

65   Shabby, shambling, an older gentleman no one, least of all yourself, wants to meet. You – after the defeat.

66   … a devilish old man of the kind who was determined to make up for the virtues of his youth.

RR: American Weather by Omeurle Alcade. When climate sparks a violent civil war in the United States, one young woman fights to stay in veterinary school.

---

67   When did I lose confidence in my words? When it sounded like I believed them.

68   The utter presumption in thinking you have anything new to say about anything.

69   Aside from a few fatal flaws – a facticity that is the flat face of didacticism, facetiousness that is the back slap of condescension, and a seriousness lacking any dimension of depth, the book under review wasn't that bad.

70   *Sign post.* Not a highway of verbal conveyances, tour of narrative features, or points along a plot but a district that could be entered and exited at any point, traversed at various paces and intensities of attention (including skips) with movement in any direction; an arrondissement of nooks, alleys, souks, small parks, shuts.

(The generating gestalt of these words being anxiety, a rasorial inability to credit or create systems and totalities. Minerva's owl takes flight at twilight with great swoops of wing; her sparrows fuss and flutter in the daylight.)

71   He was awake many hours in the night trying to formulate articulable, non-banal truths. In other words, he lost a lot of sleep, laughing.

72   Lets' speculate on the exact nature (civil/social war, bankruptcy, defeat by China?) of America's humiliation. After all, it's her last hope.

[It's hard to decipher this semi-Spenglerian prophetic morass. It seems to be saying that the best hope for America's better future arises from the possibilities presented in the working out of extreme crisis. When has that ever been true ... Rome, 44 B.C.? France, 1789? Russia 1917? Germany 1919?]

73   One wonders in which season the catastrophe will happen so that it or (depending on where it falls in the quarter) the one before is remembered, the last good spring, summer, fall, winter, framed and fabled. August 1914 all over again.

Now you might ask, how do you know all this? I know it in the usual way before and after sleeping with someone for two weeks. Funny the euphemism; not that much sleep, actually. And sure, I understand, you're not interested in editorial mechanics or bibliographical minutiae. What you really want to know is what she looked like? Ok.

The first thing you'd notice would be a helmet of dark hair, flowing, framing a long white face with deep set grey/green eyes – sea gems of unfathomable depth, the serious line of lips, her default look of almost sad expectation. You could call her "willowy" except for the vibrancy and strength of her movement, the waist that ached for an arm (yours, as you apprehended it), her voice that was low and light at the same time, her stride like a huntress, the engaging gap at the jointure of her long legs, the perfect geometries of her etceteras ... actually, I, the author can't stand this stuff. Not that it's necessarily bad but we've enough of it, millions of pages, the many hundred thousand testimonies (or testy-moanies) transcribed by the male desiring eye. Basta.

74   Record cold here, six hundred miles north in New England, it's double digits of frost with five feet of freshly fallen snow. Tonight, and in the days after, thousands of beings will quietly die in the cities and suburbs ... pigeons, sparrows, squirrels. Who ponders their fate or says a prayer? If warm in my bed, I think of them, taking comfort in the comparison, there's nothing commendable in it.

75   Nothing is crueler than snatching a creature out of its element and letting it suffocate in air. "But", it is explained "fish don't feel pain."

76   As to souls and "immortal parts", it's naive to suppose we have them as endowments. Maybe they are earned or are "remote", the operative model that of the little Martian robot/rover, relaying all the vital data of its explorations back to mission control, its self-monitoring and functional awareness the equivalent of our individual consciousness, (just) a responsive control mechanism. The real vitality of the project is a long way away. I get a similar feeling when I read slippery thinkers like Deleuze, my understanding of them, as such, occurs at a conceptual remove. Nothing personal, you understand.

[Fly that by me again?]

77   Conventional writers, despite their commitment to "realism", don't deal with the fact that most men, ages fifteen to fifty, think of women all the time by which I mean 30-40 times a day, in what can only be called pornographic terms.[12] No fiction, except pornographic fiction is as sexualized as a man's thoughts. All men know this and most women who have to deal

---

12   The rough numbers supplied are like bird-watching, an accounting of appearances, of coming into calculable consciousness, not a measurement of the totality of the phenomenon. The cited age range too is approximate. In my personal case, the age range was from eleven to sixty-two. (A precocious child, in my twelfth year, I invented my first masturbation device, consisting of a toilet paper tube, plastic bag, and vegetable oil. Subsequent models, in an era of 3D printing (itself an outmoded process by the time you read this), might have made me a millionaire.)

with them. (Not all men are pornographphillic, nor do all women resent it.) Despite being the dominate form of male consciousness as regards sexuality, its full depiction in novels is very rare, as if "good taste" in the matter guaranteed good art.

[Ever hear of Philip Roth or his suede shoe bro, John Updike? Frank Harris, John Cleveland, Sade?]

Autopornobiography

No biography, our truest history would be
a medium of harsh lighting and bare facts,
something nearer pornography, its close ups and
    sound tracks:
your sighs when you first were stripped ...
how within weeks your shy smiles became
    knowing grins
and there followed as if fast forwarding, months
    of discoveries –
kinks, stunts, rope tricks, acrobatics.

In our rich middle installment
you were almost mechanically passionate –
I see your head reeling on the pillow,
slo-mos of the way you gripped me in,
I hear your reliable cries rewinding
(that item of my pride when neighbors

stared and I knew they were thinking
"She's the loud one, the screamer. There.")

These days you parade in after your bath
and stop, powdered and perfumed, a foot from
    my face.
A pause, a space. After three thousand plus fucks,
our bodies couldn't care less but our wills are
    restive
and deeply sexed. So naturally, I drop my book,
hit some switch, touch myself and look.

78   In a sense, your life is a contrivance designed to hurt you, a completive act of formation, deformation, information. Contented people sense their depravation, which explains their drive for consummation via adulteries, high stakes gambling and various other extreme sports.

79   I avoid generalizations about the sexes as they are invariably crass excepting the truism that, in all times and places, men are responsible for 90% of the world's evil. One I would offer is that women generally prefer clean shaven men in order to make a careful assessment of their countenances and play of features. A few women prefer bearded men, seeing in them a counterpart to their own darkness. Such

women are to be avoided – especially if you are a bearded man.

80 *The difference between men and women in a nutshell.* Sentenced to be shot at dawn, most men will theorize about how much sex is possible in the interim. ("Some woman has a grudge against the warden or the judge. She's gonna make a batch of homemade explosives (ammonia and baking soda?), cart it next to this wall, set it off. I'll scurry through the breach, we'll unhitch the horses and ride to the mountains where we'll make love five times before light lines the East and the firing squad, grumbling, begins to clear the rubble. Nothing implausible about it.")

81 What's best about the Jane Austen movies: the party scenes, when the gentlemen and ladies line up for dancing and each sex pays the other objective respect.

82 Encountered in a book: "He had his way with her", a phrase which, never used these days, has acquired a dubious dignity, being *vintage*. Accurate enough about male focus and view, the drive for victory even in the lap of love, the template for all other victories. Not that that's the whole story. A woman too has her way, the way of having her way with his having his way, her positioning a strong skirmish line

to absorb his force, then joining the melee with passion and dexterity while keeping a reserve, in every sense, *in-tact*. In this shared ferocity can be found not only concord of instinct but a human sympathy; we think, "she is like that", "he is like that." And likes *that*. *Moral*: making love is not making war even when resounding with the clash of arms.

[That pun hurts.]

The Peace

Was it like this –
the concuss of the last aimed gun diminishing,
crowds surging in famous streets,
cities loud with light and victorious couplings
late the next day awakening
to find their uniforms thrown off, estranged,
the grip of orders slipped and so they rested,
entirely at ease but for their straining to find
a familiar threat in the morning's hollow.
Was it like that –
our history of inflicted defeats
ending in this miracle where we both have won
and smile like statesmen at the treaties?
Days pass in a secure peace, for instance now
as we chat, cool atop the sheets, such friends
everything can be asked, be answered

except this – Do you miss the hard times?
their fact and metaphor the minutes just before
when I sized you up, we grappled
and were merciless in our movements,
making not love but war.

83   In my naivete, I used to think the cause of bad books, art, and music was laziness or an innocent lack of talent, technical skills. In my paranoia, I now think bad art is deliberate, willed, an intended result to actualize the satisfactions of hypocrisy and "emperor's new clothes" confidence tricks. Both positions are correct. |cf.no.30|

["Actualize the satisfactions" is a vile phrase.]

84   *Outside of a dog, a man's best friend is a book* ... It was quite a relief to realize I no longer needed to worry about books or the fates of literary characters – Miss Havisham, Charlotte Stant, Lawrence Birkin, "King" Cadwallader. The case was similar to "people"; I didn't need to meet any more of them, the category was satisfied. My spirits lifted, as if I was a balloon escaped from a child's hand, wobbling into the empyrean; I felt like a young goat, skipping on the hillside. I went to a mirror to check on the change, saw the same grey hair and lined, ashen face but my ancient eyes were glittering now and gay.

[He doth profess too much, me thinks. Saturation is not satiety.]

85   For all their vanity, extravagance and (self) destructiveness, people do, in a sense, know what they are doing: they are contriving and living the drama of their lives. Because when the drama is over, what's to live for? Let me guess – grandparenthood and serenity.

[Forgetting, aren't you, sunset sex cruises?]

RR: Table for Three by Jarndyce Bloom. Lurid cases from the file of California's most famous divorce attorney.

---

86   Having committed a few crimes, (see my novel, *A Book of Emblems*, available from Amazon and fine book shops everywhere, for a lightly fictionalized account of them. *) I well understand the exculpatory disposition of the criminal mind. "First, compelled by forces and circumstance out of my control, I am not fully responsible for my bad acts. Second, it is hard for me to feel full remorse because, with the passage of time, I am not the person who did them". Here, a difficulty arises: the more he separates himself from the perpetrator, the more that detached self has an

existence of its own, looking to repay its betrayer at the same time the reformed criminal is trying to track this former avatar down to make it acknowledge a just debt of regret. Chased by something he is trying to pursue, it is no wonder that an ex-con of this better sort acquires a haunted, one might say hunted look. This isn't all bad. In certain lights it looks like dignity and a woman, somewhere, will fall for it.

(* No more than the normal quota, having bullied (slapping a lover), lied, practiced hypocrisy, envied, acted like a coward, hated. None of which concerns me; I stand by certain (still soliciting) justifications. No, what condemns me is the persons I cherished, would have given my life for, that now I could care less if they are dead or at this moment dying. What fires have I lived through to leave these hard cinders, this hollowed out heart? Such abandonments, necessary perhaps for transitionary self-preservation, seem the negation of self, the essence of anti-integrity, something eclipsing and inexplicable. The lover I slapped, yes, more than once, did I ever love that again? Maybe, maybe not. I wish her no ill will but I don't want to know if she is likely to outlive me. That would be damn annoying. |cf.no.198|

87   I recall acts from my youth I feel no attachment to, they seem like witnessed actions of another person, objects that have passed beyond my personal horizon. The reasons, excuses, justifications for these events

were more persistently possessed but they too have grown distant. Indeed, I now see the identified reasons not as valid explanations but as integral elements of the event-object, a kind of radiation, likewise lessening, a diminished glow from a disappearing isotope. The best I can do is to register these improbable deeds as my own and try to take responsibility for them – an act of will I haven't much motivation for because, really, what has it to do with me? |cf.no.110|

Before Burning the Old Letters

What is it with these strange scripts
and I don't just mean the hasty, ill formed scribal hands
but the accounts of these frantic goings-on,
the characters crammed on the letters' little stage
so free with their almost forgotten names —
the Karens, Susans, Bills —
their breakups and reconciliations,
their sudden projects and cross-country trips,
and at the center of it all
the passive-aggressive little shit
who always wants to win the girl, the job --
him, I half recognize.
But what really makes me sick
is the sense, reading between the lines,
(suddenly my eye supplies "lies")

how easily it might all have turned out differently;
for one thing, I might have died and not ended up
so wise and likewise (my current thoughts
transcribed for some later reader) wrong.

(Burning the Old letters)

Seasoning

There was delight, seeing the fire
singeing the edges like a stationer's motif,
burning the sheets behind, bursting out,
a hot mouth that ate your face of words.
My careful heels crushed the ashes.
What was left of your hundred letters?
A small square of folded paper I'd saved,
labeled "seeds from my garden-1998".
These I dropped in the hungry spring
and watched the plants thrust up and thrive.
Chives. All summer, I cropped the leaves,
sweeping heaps of pungent green
into empty Twinings tins. One plant untouched,
its blades curled into tubes, spear tipped buds
breaking into lacy butterflies of flower
that were shriveled pods before October's rains,
slashed and whipped, seeds for the next harvest.
But what of my dried spice, remains of our hot
    season?

It starts out lemony tart, ends up grit against my teeth.

This long winter I use it to season vegetables and meats.

A bitter herb, I sprinkle, I eat.

88   It's assuaging, as regards individuals one has injured, to understand it was all part of an essential education that has made one a better person; much less comforting to consider yourself a lesson session in someone else's course of improvement.

89   The exonerating declaration "I didn't deserve the dirt done to me" should always be accompanied by the trip-wired observation "Maybe I *did* deserve it."

(Or, at least "earned it" in the sense of "having become worthy of", a self-ennobling.)

Six Jisei by Howa Nessen (1625-1660?)

The third son of low ranked samurai, Howa eschewed the way of the warrior, traveling over much of Hokkaido as a mendicant poet before, in the words of *Ten Thousand Lives of the Poets*, "he rested in Kyoto." Palace rolls for eight years in the 1650's contain the name of a minor scribe named Howa, a low ranked member of the coterie of Lady Asiwasayng

(1622?-1685), likely but not proven the same person as the poet. Howa is remembered for his unprecedented composition of five *jisei* or "death poems". Otherwise, none of his poetry is preserved.

Too bad.
That morning glory
Aspired to see the moon.

With closed eyes
in the icy water, floating,
A duck — What of it?

Today is the day I die.
I have eaten enough.

I laughed
When my enemy died.
Just then –

First frost.
No cricket sings.

List of Disagreeable Things by Lady Asiwasayng

A cat that snores on the bed when it is a feline of the fifth rank and cannot be awakened so that you must listen to it all night.

Mice that make noise, having a party at 3AM that then leave dirty little calling cards for you to find in the morning.

A cat that does not lift a paw against such mice.

Flocks of robin that in winter defecate while flying so you can only go outside with an umbrella.

The whine of mosquitos.

Flowers left too long in a vase.

People who dye their hair.

A lover who is too gentle, one who is not gentle enough.

Unidentified stains on silk.

A lover quick to leave in the morning; a lover who lingers and won't let you start the day.

Treacherous lovers who smile; what are they so satisfied about?

Poets who when they read their poems sound as if they had found their words discarded in the street so they must refurbish them by rolling them around in their mouths and then articulate them like they were new or unique words – this is very disagreeable.

Those who talk constantly about the book they are writing but when you ask them when it will be completed, go silent and act as if you have committed a breach of manners.

Ladies at court who compile a list of disagreeable things – this is most disagreeable thing of all.

90   Cats in the wild never say "meow".

[Generally considered the most prefect articulation of our talented aphoristic expostulator.]

91   Admittedly, we owners over esteem our cats' abilities but this avoids the greater error of under esteeming them.

92   *Breaking news ...* the big news, concentrated in the obituary section, that death stalks the land, occasionally spills over unto the front page ("Earthquake kills hundreds in Mexico.")

93   What's most disturbing about the idea of reincarnation is that I might again have relationships with the chief reprobates I encountered in this life. Charitably regarded, they could be called "teachers'

but of the type one learns never to take another class from. Of course, I'd like to think I taught them a thing or two, too.

94   Facets of meanings, fashioned in the night, dissipate like dew jewels in the morning. Why is that?

[Because you are an idiot.]

95   *A thanks to my reviewers.* The critics have weighed in and it's not a gush, more a down piping, they've plumbed my depths and found them leaden. Oh well, I've still a flush of excitement – hope's little swirl gurgling down the drain.

96   Military systems are increasingly automated to respond against perceived tactical or strategic assault, a matter of shaving a few seconds off reaction time. As these retaliations get closer and closer to the initiating stimulus, it's only a matter of time before one of those AI minds has the thought "I can beat all rivals by being first – and doing it *now*."

97   Simonides, Nietzsche and many more minor minds are agreed – "Life is a game." But when the

only game in town is the "game of life" (containing and conditioning all others), is it really right to call it a game?

98   The victims of low to middle grade crimes reflexively strike back with accusation: "how could you, by what right, how dare you" that at its heart is a form of resentment, hardly a noble feeling. The perpetrators have successfully enveloped their victims in yet another dimension of injury. (Victims of higher crimes are dead or so damaged in their selfhood they are incapable of response.[13])

99   The better of the two ways way out of this gyre of self-degradation, the sublimation of saints and martyrs, is not one I have followed. The other method, revenge, is often right at hand but of such incalculable inaccuracy (initiating endless chains of collateral damage) that the victim is restrained by the one thing that sustains him in his state of abasement – a sense of justice.

100   That lovely lily in the field. Is it beautiful even if not one being (I've no doubt bees have a sense of

---

[13] Though, famously, Tolstoy records Prince Andrei's wife, Lise, reproaching him for his lack of affection with her dead countenance.

beauty) perceives it? (An important question, not asked for the first time.)

101 Simone Weil, various saints, and gurus, all desire a kind of purity, truth, and knowledge not possible in the realm of normal life. They say your attachment to the mess of existence is just that – grasping, ignorance, and in a sense, laziness. But consider the sun rising on a new day, on the multitude of lives with their labors, desires, loves and shames. What single truth would you assign to them, what one path should they follow?

[How about that old chestnut – rub it and it shines – "Be kind."]

102 Matched up the First to the First, the Second to the Second, and so forth, only musicologists would consider Brahms' symphonies superior to Schumann's which, with their quirky invention, colorful mood swings and overall air of nobility, are preferred by appreciators and musicians. Yet in the period of my devastations, Schumann's fundamental goodness and decency seemed impossibly remote, melodies from fairy land. Those months, how many times did I play the only music that gave expression to my state, the third movement of Brahms' third. Yes, I'm burnt out on Brahms as if his music were a

course of chemo; a scalding treatment that can't be repeated.

We enter the airy oblong box,
Symphony Hall's expectant space
framed by tons of brick, plaster, iron,
sitting atop 20,000 white pine pilings
driven deep into the muddy bottom.
"Check the ticket", we are high up
Second Balcony left, 22 and 23 B
and soon on the edge of our seats
to see the conductor and because this is exciting
   stuff –
Schumann's trombone golden "Rhinish",
a bright island of sound surrounded
by the city's traffic, static (white noise of the stars)
and eighty meters beneath us
the waters of an ancient lake,
cold, still, color of slate.

103   Mice are lovely with their tope colored bodies, bright black pin eyes, exquisite ears, delicate feet, their tiny teeth – just like us they have enamel and gums. Which hasn't stopped me from setting snap traps that tear their heads off. I'm reminded of the writer Beatrice Hastings who, old, sick and alone, gassed herself with her pet mouse carefully cupped in her hand. It was much loved.

104 We can recognize the evil we intend but what about the evil we unwittingly promote? Consider the fair-minded, well-educated, eminently judicious professors who turn down the application of the stilted provincial sketch artist. He's not talented enough for the big academy, and slots are limited; he is never going to be as good as the other students and, as an unhappy misfit, is all but certain (as we know from every aspect of his biography) to fail or drop out. The good professors are acting correctly. Yet in rejecting young artist-aspirant Adolf Hitler, they are making a prodigious mistake.

(It is possible that with just a semester of technical training, Hitler might have acquired enough skill and discipline to support himself as moderately successful petit bourgeois – with a hobby of radical politics. We can't know. What we do know is that a direct line exists from the "nein" on his application to the trains running to the death camps. Who takes responsibility for that? No good citizen.)

RR: First degree. When a literary authority is found dead at UVa, police are baffled. As the investigation develops, it turns out there are as many motives as suspects for offing the "kindly" old prof. (Published in Britain as "The Case of Dr Casey.")

105   The American sublime: another day without thinking.

106   *Camp versus Kampf.* My child, these art objects (Mozart, for example) are the toys of culture – may they bring you joy.

And those others?

Bludgeons, at best blades compounded from pain and that give pain, weapons that wound the wielders, not playthings.

[Pseudo Nietzschean clap-trap. Proof that every toke of the aphorism inclines one to megalomania. Ecce Homomonomaniac..]

107   The charm and ingenuity of Mozart's compositions don't quite overcome the detractions of his musical rhetoric – every bar expressing "Mozart". His music is worse than it sounds.

[For you, the crucial thing about music (and art, generally) is the expression and appreciation of personality, a doctrine notoriously propounded (refuted?) by the critic Victor Dogge who wrote, in 1950, "By this dogma, we should prefer the works of "good guy" Rockwell over those of cut-throat Caravaggio."]

108   The incomplete presentation of an idea is often more effective than its exhaustive realization. The appreciator is left with a task to perform, to continue working on what appears to be a sketch, to think it through to the end and to that extent, make it his own.

109   However much one might admire Nietzsche's thought, it ultimately amounts to the usual words, words, words. For philosophy in action, nothing beats his saving a cart horse from being whipped even if, just technically, it contradicts more than a few passages in his texts.[14]

[No contradiction. By then, he was nuts.]

110   Any diligent and fair-minded researcher writing a screen play of my life in my twenties, could justly, drawing from the facts, depict me as a brute and a fool. Knowledge, however, of the internal and hidden "quantum physics" of relations governing myself and others involved with me in that decade would generate another impersonation entirely.[15] Hence my skepticism of all biography. This inferred "deep

---

14   See the numerous anti-pity rants in *Daybreak*.

15   In moments of self-reflective non-action, I felt situated in an identity. I lost this sense of self-location, in activity. Call it the principle of "individual complementarity": it was possible to have knowledge of location or velocity but not both at the same time.

physics" is still an actual if practically inaccessible *history*. Beneath that is the dark matter of human interaction, a thing beyond all kenning that Freud was right to posit but wrong to describe.

[Good biographies present the nexus of nature and nurture, the panorama of persons born into histories they make their own and alter, the interaction of wills like ripples of raindrops in a pond. In this objectification of lives in a way we can never achieve in our own case, the deepest lessons learned are not about others but about ourselves.]

(Sure. Provided one learns to read between the lies.) |cf.no.87|

RR: The Information Man by Tod Alcott. Ashbury Bloom, senior reference librarian at the New York Public Library, is the "got to go to guy" gone to by actors, financiers, doctors and media prognosticators for all their info needs. An importer-exporter of refined confidences, a trader in daily trusts and bespoke hog-wash, Bloom's reign as the king of information is suddenly interrupted when a grey garbed stranger assails him for violation of the "Protocols of Odin."

111   The Americans and Chinese think they can avoid the "Thucydides trap", not knowing it has the power to bend every action away from it, towards it. (Examples: both sides agree to zones of control to facilitate passage in the South China sea. Then a ship or plane trespasses in one of the zones by error, a violation more incendiary than one when no demarcations existed. Or, as has already happened, America stops selling quality arms to Taiwan in order not to anger China, weakening Taiwan so that China is tempted into invasion and the Americans militarily respond. History is a trap that always snaps.

("The hounds are playing in the courtyard, and the hare is already running through the forest but it will not escape them." Kafka.)

112   The more one's friends die, the more death seems just something you (ought to) do.

113   Heavily sedated on his deathbed, he said "I don't quite have a handle on this.", last words consonant with the circumspection and graciousness of his life. (The deceased: some are mourned – and that's it, they are not missed. Others are missed and never intensely mourned. He was best of men. With every breath of the living who loved him, he is mourned and missed.)

114 The evening after being informed of my friend's death, I couldn't stop thinking of instances of his unkindness; one cutting remark, one joke at my expense, one social brush off; three incidents in a thirty-year relationship of reciprocal sympathy and generosity. It is, no doubt, to my credit that I can submit to public exposure my contemptible pettiness.

[Not to mention heavy weight irony.]

115 These days, I sometimes awake in the middle of the night, terrified of dying. I try to stifle all thought, lessen my breathing and lie very quiet, putting my head under the blankets. Here's safety I think, and as the years go by, I'm getting better at it – playing dead.

116 Two years after she'd died, grief had subsided and I had returned to the normal rhythm of things, the dance of life. The difference from before was the sense that I was waltzing above a void – don't look down, nothing supports us. Yet there is a validity to natural vitality, the impulsive exertions propelling us through our element, like birds in flight. We were meant for this: living.

RR: Falling under by Joan Smith. A young woman reads aloud to a 105-year-old man as she considers his proposal of marriage.

---

117   After the rape, I could be bold because nothing now much mattered.

[Interesting. Were you the victim or the perp?]

118   Suddenly, like a change of seasons, the glances that once were force fields drawing one to "The Other" became nothing more than people using their eyes.

119   *Cinema review*. If you look for it, you see how silent films got it right: the silence between lovers is more important than the talk.

120   We're all in the same boat – the lifeboat. Every sea-farer knows or should know the cardinal rule – no fighting in the lifeboat. (Save that for the shore.)

Poets Corner

(Sponsored by Doc Nelson's Omni-Balsamic Priapic Reinvigorator)[16]

[I had rather be a kitten and cry mew
Than one of these same meter ballad-mongers;
I had rather hear a brazen canstick turn'd,
Or a dry wheel grate on the axle-tree;
And that would set my teeth nothing on edge,
Nothing so much as mincing poetry:
'Tis like the forced gait of a shuffling nag.]

121 *Poetry.* "Men die miserably every day from lack of what is found there." If so, the producers and pushers of adulterated poems deserve incarceration or worse. (What they usually get is prizes, an insidious poison for which there is no antidote.)

122 If five thousand American poets booked passage on one of those hotel/casino type ocean liners and sailed permanently over the horizon, what effect would this have on contemporary culture?

[Inquiring minds also want to know: were you born mean or made mean by events?]

(It is an exact *irony* that I could have been – and often have been (mis)taken for – a nice guy. Not a hypocrite,

---

16 Contains alcohol. In the event of intentional ingestion, do not drive or operate machinery.

I've done everything I could in this work to expunge my good reputation.)

123   At some point American poetry's traditional inattention to verbal particularity and its cruder rhetorical registers combined with the abstruseness of the "New Poetics" (itself a rip-off of art's abstract expressionism) to produce a poetry of exceptional _____.

(Choose one)
Futility opaqueness meaninglessness ugliness self-indulgence pretentiousness crudity

[Yet collections of poetry, even as described, are superior to dictations of aphorisms which, anteriorly, are condescendingly preemptive and posteriorly resistant to discourse. In the words of the critic, Lilly Marlene "The aphorism *always* sounds like *that*." [17]]

124   American poetry has finally achieved its retrograde escape velocity – it's never going to get any better, the literary engine being stoked by teachers, critics, and publishers who can do no better than promote writing as bad or worse than their own.

---

[17]   Marlene, Lilly, *Under the Lamplight and Other Readings Behind the Lines,* Verso, 2002. See also her *Contestations*, *Cahier*, Universitee du Montgomery IV, Avranches, 2004.

In technical terms: negative feedbacks, systemic degradation, downward spiral. It's that simple. (But some people won't be pleased. Take Ange Mlinko – viewed in one intense enactment ("take"). She's clever, learned, a verb bender/blender, punslinger, allusional, rhymes when she wants to, someone you retread to reread to make sure you haven't stepped over a joke you should have tripped (a foot trap, pray), nothing plain said, so many vertiginous spins even the OED you carry, required kit, won't steady you. Too cute, too assured, succulent fruit of many tenured years, grants and leaves, this is a poetry for the bright and young. There's a word how and why it strikes them – it's dumb.)

[Not a generous type, the best compliment he could serve up to handout was a back hand. He'd done better to have said less and quoted Moore, "I, too, dislike it." Instead, one is reminded of the chorus of a not quite popular (it was caviare to the general) song – "No known harm in a Cassius look, hungry and lean but the wide world over, it's mean to be mean, mean to be mean, mean to be mean …"]

125   If the point of poetry is to stimulate emotion and invoke pity, my poem "*My Poor Sick Squirrel*" (that's it) is a fine one. If additionally, the aim is to report and indict injustice, "*My Poor Sick Abused Squirrel*" will do. Ninety percent of all American poems yet published in the 21st century are of this type, with the

poet usually impersonating the squirrel. These poems are admirable in every way except for their lack of verbal intelligence. Even the mildest critic should be moved because the unnamed topical victim of such work, stunned, bludgeoned and beaten down, is poetry itself.[18]

126 Poetry is never there (here), immediate in full dimensionality; it requires considerable mediation, conduction by consciousness through time so that every word has to deserve and overcome the inertia of this labor which is why it is harder to write a good poem than paint a good painting and why there is much more bad poetry than good art when there is no lack of good art. In a poem, every word resonates with every other, dead words are more than particularly damaging, they void whole networks of interchange. In painting, you can always smudge a blot and the greatest masters have.

[Name one such painting or master. Oh, Blotero.]

127 I have no attraction to trash heaps. But if you were to tell me that the one on the corner had gems buried within it, the situation would be unhappily

---

18 For a provocative, highly theoretical and arguably effective defense of poems such as "My Sick Squirrel' (that's it) see *Poetry and Mind*, by Laurent Dubreuil, Fordham University Press, 2018.

altered. I could no longer ignore the mound and might feel an obligation, without necessarily acting on it, to rake through the muck to rescue any items of value. The name of the trash heap is "contemporary poetry". It grows ever higher. Good citizens pass by and pay it no heed.

[This little allegory would be perfected if our author told us about his own pail, brought to the heap, and how he regarded it. Was it muck, dust, pretty stones, jewels?]

128   The advice "keep writing" nearly always emanates from prose writers. For poets, the best advice is to read, think, live, play with words in your head – and be patient.[19] Wait for the poem to arrive. Nothing is better guaranteed to give poor results than writing poetry to write poetry, a practice responsible for 90% of mediocre poetry or 80% of all poems where 10% fail for other reasons and 10% are something you might want to read.

[No Muse is good Muse? Prosaically considered, how do you arrive at these figures?]

---

19   People were given the choice between becoming kings or couriers. Now everyone knew that being a king was no fun and quoted Shakespeare on the subject. So, they all decided to be courier/heralds because they'd get to wear fancy uniforms, ride fine horses, blow horns and stay at the best inns. Accordingly, the world is full of couriers who dash about shouting to each other messages which, since no kings reign, are trivial. (after Kafka)

128a *Tip for writers:* Never use one word when two or three will do. The reading mind, like the seeing eye, desires beauty, interest, complexity. It wants poetry even in its prose.

[Er, you're saying something as simple as
"Westron wynde, when wyll thow blow
The smalle rayne downe can rayne?" isn't beautiful?]

(No, I'm saying it isn't simple.)

129 Having read hundreds of critical books on contemporary poetry (a hobby horse no more frivolous than any other), I find them of a consistent, indeed formulaic character. A smart teacher-critic goes to work on the poetic productions of an *expressive person* and discovers, articulates, enhances or imagines interesting qualities in that work. Showing the poet good makes the critic even better. If the reply is made "Yes, that's what criticism is for", note what is missing – negative, comparative or dismissive commentary. Anyone by this non-zero-sum practice can be and has been promoted into the modular pantheon – Berryman, Williams, Ashbury, Graham, S. Howe, Levine and fifty others. This type of criticism is simply a "pump-up mechanism" whose hydraulic effect is a downward spiraling, a flush, or more technically, a self-staging, self-serving exercise in positivity. It's like going to a winetasting in a second-rate region – Virginia, Texas, Missouri, where each sample brims

with more superlatives than the one before and the first was "a prize winner in its class." (As was *Stewball*, who was a racehorse but not a very good one, a country track claimer, finishing in the money four out of twenty-three starts. He always drank wine, a problem in his training. Not to be confused with *Skewball*, the celebrated Hibernian champion though both were skewbald (pied) horses.) [A *tour de horse*?]

SCREWBALL

THE RACE-HORSE

"In art, it is right to speak of value because art is mediated by a subjectivity that is limited and rationed by death. Every art work says 'I'm good, no?' – a

question addressed to a comportment that knows what and how to value." (Adorno, AT 1997, p.262)

[Since you began this with a mention of hobby reading, let me tell you, you'd have had more fun booking a geriatrical Carnival Cruise; the going-ons on that boat, from the elite in the Updike suites to the near stiffs in steerage, the continuous Flibansarin/Viagrow fueled orgies, like a floating terrarium brimmed with humping turtles, disgusting, but nay – what's true too – pathetic/heroic in the old Adam and Eve way…] |cf.no.85|

130   Everyone knows the secret place, the space of sexual desire and fantasy where words have erotic power. Here the poet tries on various outfits the way a manly man puts on a lacy garter belt, a woman her strap-on. Every (real) poem (and poet) is whipped into shape running the gauntlet from fetish to finish.

131   Poetry has a kind of value as one of the few non-detritus items you can't give away. You can stand on a street corner and people that will accept (as talismans or curiosities) old bolts, bent nails, used rubber bands, tangled string will politely decline your free verse.

132 Generally speaking, cowboy poets are to be avoided. As poets, they are serious about their works (*My Little Horse, What These Boots Have Seen, Down in Old Laredo, Arizona Senorita and A Lonesome Credo*); as cowboys, they can beat you up if you don't like them.

If boots could talk, what these boots have seen
The many years, both fat and lean.
From the wilds of Wyoming, to the saloons of old Laredo,
My little horse knows our lonesome course,
Sheds a mare's pure tear whilst I recite the Cowboy Credo.

"A man's got to do what a man's got to do
Make his vows and always follow through.
Never forget the last, straying steer
And though you may feel it, never show fear.
That good horse and a trusty gun,
 A woman's true love, if you have just one
You've done well, my son.
And if God bless you with all three
You're as rich as any man can be…"
That's part one of the Cowboy Credo.

Fancy boys back east, they carp and jive
Who never skinned a rattlesnake live …

Or lassoed a cactus for a prickly margarita
Or duffed theirs hats with an eye for a chat
With Arizona senoritas who never met or hope to
That punslinger, wily Black Bart Jean-Paul
   Jacques Derrida.

If you are finding this all pretty lame (and only at
   Credo pt. two)
I'd refer you to what's better but somewhat the
   same:
The parody works of Sheriff Clive "Boomeroo"
   James.[20]

(A friendly if forthrightly facetious salute to the cowboy poem, any middling example of which exceeds the poems published the *New York Times Magazine's* weekly poetry showcase feature in the period 2013 to mid-2018.)

Envoi. I used to run after the good poets, I wanted to be in their place. The separation may have been great but I knew my strength; I might get there, with work and grace. Now, I'm welded to this earth. The distances are astronomical, the constellations clear and fixed. But true, too – you can't see yourself – from space.

---

[20] Boomeroo, a male kangaroo. See James' *Peregrine Prykke's Pilgrimage Through the London Literary World* and other brilliant parodies.

133 Boxing is "manly" in that the fighter knows that in giving a blow, he will likely receive one. My poems are poised, unflinched, as foils to my critique and myself shown in other relations to have been a fool that others might be known for what they were, which was worse.

[You're saying a joker trumps a knave? Not in most games of poke her.]

134 There are liars and – far more contemptible – there are lying liars. You might wonder, how does a *lying* liar lie? By tactically telling the truth. |cf.no.5|

RR: Life sentences. By John Johnson. Serving two life terms for double murder, California inmate Johnson finds redemption in creative writing. His poems of anger and forgiveness, hope, and despair will transport you to new frontiers of compassion.

---

135 I enjoyed being an intellectual outsider; the view was wider and the air fresher there.

136 *The longer one lives, the more acutely one perceives life's deeper patterns, the working out of*

below the surface forces, the fulfillments of destiny. Something to it, perhaps, but my considered diagnosis of this development is *nostalgic effects* of brain shrinkage and vascular constriction.

137   How strange that a long friendship should hinge upon one specific expectation which, if disappointed, effectively relegates "friend" to "acquaintance."

138   The answer to the question "How does music (Beethoven's quartets) have meaning?" will go a great way toward answering the question "How does abstract art (Tanguy, say) have meaning?"

[And vice versa? Gibberish both ways.]

139   Yes, I drink too much and I do it self-consciously and calculatingly as a matter of risk. It's much less expensive and environmentally damaging than mountain climbing, auto racing or any other form of glamourous hazard. I sit in my chair, swirl another little finger's depth of scotch and savor the danger.

140   Three days without water and the nice neighbors of this leafy suburb would be at each other's throats which is why I support my constitutional right to bear

an 18th century musket, a weapon entirely adequate for home defense and difficult to criminalize.

(Difficult because the methodical motions required for loading inhibits the committing of spur of the moment crimes, such as the impromptu killing of wives).

RR: Blueline Highways by Bradely Karlott. Laid off from his job in the financial sector after a merger, a New York stock broker draws on his savings to fund a six-month trip along secondary roads to discover forgotten regions of the country – and his heart. "A profoundly American peregrination."—*The New York Venue of Books*.

---

141   His "late style" had acquired, from inactivity, the sedimentary clarity and minor effervescence of a low-grade sparkling wine.

[Whine?]

142   Dan Dennett strikes me (and many of his professional peers) as the preeminent philosopher of the last half century, admirable for his conceptual grasp, acuity and focus in argument. Doggedness and a lack of poetry are not bad qualities in a critical thinker. But

after much reading of him, one begins to suspect that his lack of "lightness" is not just loss of faculty but of a vital facility, that in his tool box for wrenching answers, a required spanner is missing. Always he seems seem to know the answers or know he *will* know them and this surety is ultimately undermining, as if you were listening to the most comprehending and continuous of straight men and it dawns on you that you are never going to get the punch line or like watching a cartoon character, say Wyllie Coyote, a figure totally in command of his brief, confidently striding forth – twenty, thirty feet from the cliff edge now and over thin air. (Yet surely Dennett is correct: the "problem of consciousness' is being solved by physicalist-functionalist science. The only caveat comes from history; classical physics was satisfactorily explanative until by the very research exertions of conventional experimenters, the frame of inquiry "deepened and expanded" to a point where the classical model needed to be superseded. (In biographical terms, the sexual knowingness of our youth is seen to be partial over and against our deeper knowledge of human and evolutionary biology.)[21] In the long run, I expect science will reach conclusions on brain/mind that Dennett, in his current physicalist-functionalist frame of mind, would find astonishing, his astonishment turning out to be more than "5.645 microflux intakes (at .283732 millivolts.) of serotonin at sodium

---

21 "The wren goes to 't, and the small gilded fly does lecher in my sight." – The botanist, Leroy Leer.

positive aspect receptors in brain regions 869-871, recursive", a mechanic's checklist that is all his current philosophy allows.)[22]

143   Exposure to an environment too rich in masterpieces results in the "too many Parthenons phenomenon". Spectators grow jaded, unappreciative and art declines. Also negative, too many Pizza Huts so that a Parthenon is lost amid the plastic vortex. Best is a rich mix of Pizza Huts and Parthenons. In 21st century America, the landscape is more complex: a few Parthenons, many Pizza Huts but also bespoke steak houses with columns and pediments, not to mention numerous half-Tudor car dealerships. The conservatives who bemoan the lack of quality and the optimists who laud the possibilities are both right and both wrong. Aside from that, what's to be said? Silence supplies a default refinement. (This is a parable.)

---

[22] 'In these new fields of experience, opened by modern refinements in the art of experimentation, we have met with many great surprises and even been faced with the problem of what kind of answers we can receive by putting questions to nature in the form of experiments … demanding a radical revision of the foundation for the unambiguous use of our most elementary physical concepts." – Niels Bohr, *Atomic Physics and Human Knowledge,* (1963). Bohr is a remarkably lucid writer on these issues.

144   A no doubt necessary supposition (in 2018), an artist thinking his or her installation (bricks in a sandbox, piled up cushions, a video monitor with camera that displays the observed observer spliced with snippets from *The Sea Hawk* and *Robin Hood*) is more interesting aesthetically than the fire code mandated extinguisher in the gallery corner. Nothing to get upset about only give the red canister its due. (Surely someone already has, displaying a standard fire extinguisher in a white room and sporting a catchy name – "Anti-Prometheus" or "Wellington at Waterloo." "The New" always flaunts its mixed plumage: shock/schlock.)

145   American writers aren't readers. Their writing provides the evidence. Of course, they naturally reply "We're *writers*, not readers." Likewise, most painters assert "we are creators, not connoisseurs" which explains why much of what passes as "the new" is simply the reinvention of themes and effects already devised by the more studious artists of the past.

146 Only in the performance of their practice are artists superior to average persons who invest their best intelligence in parenting, careers and the usual business of living. What's left of their brainpower is readily satisfied by Jamil Johnson's *Street Talk'n* rather than Beethoven's late quartets, *Hamilton* rather than *Hamlet*, *Star Wars* over *Smiles of a Summer's Night*, John Gresham, not John Donne. For over a hundred years artists have understood that the chief audience of their elite art is other artists, the range of whose response is well known to them. Confronted by a rival's new work, any artist's reaction is less "admire and abide with" than "bury", an internment typically effected by the presentation of their own latest creation. This explains much about modern art – it's o'er hasty over production, its reactionary self-entitlement glossing over deep grained resentment at its own existence.

147 [Nobody liked his little bracketed asides, they seemed snide and arrogant. Articulating both a position and its opposite, he was asserting his perspectival superiority. It was a way of bullying his readers and at the root of it all was the usual distasteful insecurity.]

(Lacking any ambition [that's a virtue?] and with no brimming sense of his talent, he nonetheless did think of the book as a bracketed remark, with all the pride of an aside, upon the entire corpus of contemporary American whatever.)

Hank hardly noticed the rough oscillations of the train as it sped through the long section without stops between Brookline and Chestnut Hill. So fixed was his attention on the image of race horses in his hand, the shaking registered only n the swing of his thought—that if one forgot or didn't know the entire history of Art from Lascaux Cave to Picasso (these the terminal points of his mental arc), the small drawing on flashy card, was, in its way, a masterpiece: the hunched-up jockeys, the stretching thoroughbred necks, the tangle of equine legs – was this not realism of an acutely expressive kind and really, a winner?

148   Remorse is the rarest of human elements. Pity, an abstraction which can be extended to objects, animals, and even enemies, is much more common. We rejoice in our transgressions, in triumphing over a rival (especially if a friend), and take delight akin to the sexual in "getting away with it", generating an irresistible surge of self-justification. Remorse in the average person is roughly proportionate to the amount of gold they wear (a fourth of an ounce in a finger's ring) compared to their body weight or to the number of old Nazis, two or three, who on the 20th anniversary of the Fuhrer's victory would have felt a kind of nostalgia for the missing Jews.

149   Even if our death is extended and not instantaneous, our experience of dying is a lived abstraction of weakness, disability and pain. We best understand the annihilating nature of death in perceiving the deaths of (loved) others, resulting in a sense of loss so severe it obliterates our normal self and we become, as near as it is possible to be, a void.

(How clever I was, investing in only two or three friends, sparing myself the insolvencies of their deaths. How good of me, to have saved potential friends from mine. For even assuming that grief is proportionate to engagement, they still would not have gotten their "money's worth" to cover the rupture. I find myself small minded, ungenerous, leery of involvement, a narrowly self-sufficient man too proud – of what? – of having escaped poverty – another poverty. (A dreamy, reading, rainy-day boy, poor at sports, startled by bugs bumping the window, who fancied he'd grow into a military hero.)

["Dreamy" sounds like a code word, the description conjuring a *koan. What is the sound of one stick rubbing? Wank, wank.*]

150   Generally speaking men come in two flavors: babies and bullies. To further observe that the babies can act like bullies and the bullies like babies is to be specific enough to describe 90% of all cases.

151 The refined critic Georg Steiner thinks the great age of literature is over. It is also pretty clear he finds significant gratification in being one of the last *litterateurs*. Granted, being last has a status that rivals being first even if the category is always more populated that one suspects – consider the last 5000 Confucian scholars after Mao, the last ten thousand passenger pigeons, etc. In this sense, I am the last of the encyclopedically well-read American authors and I can hardly express my delight in being unread, the satisfaction of being unknown or the high pride that accompanies the sense of one's opinions being utterly insignificant. The perversity of these notions is a saving grace; only the successful, such as Steiner, can be smug.

[The best response to such posturing is metaphorical: the last mandarins (oranges) in the batch are usually spoiled and smashed. Such "notions" could only be gracious if they are unproclaimed.]

152 America's election of Trump was "world historical" in this sense: since the promulgation of stupidly violates one of nature's sternest injunctions, the rest of the world expects America to suffer a just punishment. If it doesn't, people will justly cultivate a permanent resentment against us, a kind of back-up retribution.

RR: The Dawn's Early Dimming by Whitley Bromine. A human-alien hybrid grows up in the United States and becomes President only to discover that to win a human woman's love, he must betray the extra-terrestrials' grand plan. (Soon to be major motion picture starring Justin Bieber and Vicky Pelthrow).

153   A cheerful and, on the whole, fortunate child, I matured into a young adult two of whose dominate characteristics were unreflective hopefulness and attunement to fidelity, qualities that provided their own proof (or at least inhibited their contradiction) so that I assumed they were norms or at least standards of humanity. I lived half my life before I determined they were just personal quirks or worse: watered down or vaccine versions of stupidity and lethargy.[23] |cf.no.175|

154   Agatha Christy's "Miss Marple", who doesn't prevent catastrophe (murder) but always achieves justice, is a more plausible figure for me to venerate than Christ who, come to think of it, might not be a bad first century detective – aloof, uncanny, knowing, half in trouble with the police (the Romans) and with

---

23   The rest of the story? In good time, my disease discovered its vector, my anxiety found its fulfilling object, my lapping erosion its seismic source.

more than a few femme-fatale pals. "Jesus Christ, private eye" has, as they say "legs."

[Not in Catholic countries or the Bible Belt, Bub.]

155 *Dreamlight.* It was the first day of class for the law seminar "East German Property Law". Present were about 12-15 of us, smart, eager in that law school way. The professor, an old guy in a tweed coat who looked like William Faulkner was passing out shot glasses, saying "You all are going to NEED this." The glasses were frosted with dust.

156 He knew he was middle aged when, after experiencing disappointment and betrayal, elation and fulfillment, he began to anticipate death as the only thing that might surprise him, having only known life.

(The type who wondered, if at the end, he'd prefer a taste of cheese to seeing a friend.)

Now there came into his acoustic focus the surf-like bass booming from the plugged-in punk ahead of him, an annoyance which in the moment of his pleasant mood he was able to transpose into a drum roll of progress; the throb of a steam engine, the pulse of victory. He wasn't really here on the hard seat between the all too known destinations, home and his job in Newton. He was a locomotive still in the long station of "last night", picking up power, just pulling out. From the moment last night he had looked at it, he had known the ticket was a winner.

157 Organized Tibetan Buddhism, according to Buddhist scholar June Campbell, has oppressed women and the peasantry for hundreds of years. Even the most effective of "special" meditative practices isn't going to neutralize all that bad karma. At best, life and after life, the monks are barely keeping their heads above the depths of animal rebirth. They are never going to break their cycle of karmic debt. What they need is just one additional rebirth – a "born againing" in the love of Christ who has, on the cross, already paid for all their sins and eradicated all bad karma. I have no problem prescribing peculiarities of one religion to fix the peculiarities of another – *it's all made-up anyway*. However, good intentions count for nothing in these matters and (nearly) all faiths cheerfully condemn reformers to a canonical version of hell.

RR : Walter's World. By Walter. Supposed diary-memoir of a quantum computer 'Walter' and some Californian friends who took over the world when no one was looking. Fiction or non? You decide.

---

158   The variety and beauty in the world we love is based on death. The individual must die that Life might live. In this may be some comfort; people have always sacrificed themselves to protect and promulgate something better than themselves – their families, nation, culture and really, there is no greater good than life itself.

159   *Three dialogues with St. Simone: "Impossible to forgive anyone who has harmed us if this degrades us. We must rather think that it has not degraded but revealed our true level."* At this true level, remote from pride and personality, we are unbroken.[24]

(Of course, victims will always blame themselves for not being more vigilant, especially in instances of personal betrayal. But this is wrong. There is no shame in trusting friends; the ignominy would be in suspecting

---

24   This aspect of 'unbrokenness' is touched on in my prose poems, "The Apology"–which actually won some kind of a prize.

In the crowded diner when you said, practically out of the blue,
"I'm sorry I hurt you" it was as if amid the nicked mugs and clattering plates

you were giving me a porcelain cup, something fluted, delicate,
a gift long overdue, as if I cupped it my hands and pressed and pressed

wanting to show what I felt and thought was left – shards and cuts.

And when what was held, words, did not break, what seemed fragile were hands,

yours – that had been busy with little bags of sugar, untouched upon the table.

them. One was simply mistaken and this mistake is minor compared to the success of giving the traitors scope so that they unmask themselves as creatures for whom betrayal was either easy or hard. If easy, they are simply vile, if hard, they are slightly less contemptible but also more stupid for having to work at it.)

"Evil is monotonous in exactly the same way as what is imaginary is, like fictitious happenings entirely invented by children." This encapsulates my criticism of most literary fiction: the freedom of the form results in the triviality of the product, at least in the hands of aesthetic adolescents. (Two aspects must be mastered: form and content (that are one) and the time comes when it must be a new mastery. The nineteen-century novel had a good run but after 1914 it was no longer vital, if remaining viable. (See any recent *New York Times Book Review* section.)

[And yet, I think the only way to test the truth value of your apothems would be to substantiate them as characters working through situations, *a particular accelerator*, or fiction. Novels, generally, are better epistemic systems than philosophical opera.]

"With every second, time is taking someone to the unendurable." – a reason to be kind. My neighbor, a mild, slight, middle-aged schoolteacher, came home one winter evening to be murdered by an acquaintance of her teenage daughter, waiting in the house. One hopes she was rendered unconscious before she had time to

think about the fate of her child but life is seldom that neat. The person ahead of me in the line or that I pass on the street – they have survived or won't survive what?

The entertaining thing had been the small domestic treachery. After the second glass, a dry rosé, and before putting on the Brahms serenade, these little pennants fluttering in the falling night of afterwork fatigue, Susan having excused herself from the table, it was then he had fished out the ticket from his pocket, the ticket "officially mailed" to him as an "approved lottery promotion of the Commonwealth" and scratched it. The little particles of grey dust, soiling fingertips, catching under his nails, were the very substance of human duplicity – light stuff to be blow away in the seconds before Susan's return. It was worth, signified by a green appearing horse, $1000 and it was all his ...

160 The world rolls on, takes no notice of your injury-injustice, the micrometrical grit of it, because if it did, it would have to take notice of everyone else's, a weight of irreversible impedance and abrasion. |cf.no.46|

161 Imagine you are given a great gift but with the stipulation it cannot be refused or traded away and that you, not some agent, are fully responsible for

its care. Suddenly possessed of a yacht, a chateau, a thoroughbred horse, your life is going to change. Along with new possibilities, come new responsibilities. With the imposed conditions, one is not likely to thank one's benefactor. This is not a rare occurrence; every passing minute some person gives another an unsupportable truth.

RR: The Sussex Rex by Anne Peachey. When a young woman American decides to take up ethnology and track down the legendary golden dragon of Sussex, she excites fear and suspicion in a traditional English village when pub owners, afraid she will demystify the beast, organize to revoke her passport.

---

162 George Steiner is an admirable critic and writer but reading his short autobiographical volume *Errata*, one quickly gets surfeit of his triumphing over every experience and testifying to it in exquisitely turned out verbiage. Never, not even in Nabokov, has a first sexual intercourse been presented so smugly. Buster, trust me, nobody cares about your first fuck, or – yes, I get the message – your first (or subsequent) betrayal either.

163 *Whether report.* This chill spring, it is hard to tell if it is cherry blossom petals or snowflakes swirling in the gusts of wind.

164   It is not unpleasant to have a slight fever that lets you lie back and watch your thoughts arise and change like clouds on a hot summer day.

165   Early June 2017: the happiest time of my life, excepting episodes of sexual success in youth, when, in one week, I finished a book, the baby wrens fledged from the bird box I'd made and fireflies, like promethean sparks, rose at twilight from the deep Virginian verdure. (The next year, the same thing – and not as good.)

[Warning: may contain Fine Writing. See, for indications and directives, no.33]

(The trees and shrubs are coves, a backdrop with dimensions of shadow even as night falls, the lawn stretching before it, a stage the fireflies appear on by rising, the flashes their speaking parts, illuminations not simultaneous but with micro-seconds of interval – repartee, a witty, refined comedy of the sexes (Sheridan rather than Shakespeare), the best of light divertissements though the bugs take it, like all actors, very seriously – it's their life.[25])

---

[25] As a kind of cotillion, *Much Ado About Nothing* would seem to theatrically qualify (as that mechanical and bitter comedy *Shrew* does not) but the play makes disquieting stabs at seriousness as when Beatrice suddenly bids Benedict "to kill Claudio" and she means it, a slash so fast playgoers don't get it, as if their heads had been cut off but it has only registered as a funny surge of nerve so that they die laughing.

RR: A Trailing Net by Toby Jones. A divorced man with a shady past moves to a small New England village to give his teen-age daughter a fresh start but her relationship with the local fishing warden leads her to discover the truth about her dad's severed thumb.

166   The would-be writer needs to suffer a catastrophe that not only damages his well-being but his very being, his cohesion as a person. It must be irremediable. He can then spend the rest of his life attempting what repair he can, complaining about in his art. |cf.no.17|

167   She inquired of my friend "Your friend Page, why does he always have such a goofy grin on his face. Is he okay mentally?" The fact was, she was beautiful and I just responded with joy whenever I saw her but I could see her point. After her complaint I made a point of never smiling like that again. I'd be satisfied the hard stare of desire which was unlikely to be misinterpreted even if made me look murderous.

167   It's hard to forgive liars, not because they have pursued or achieved their selfish agenda but because they have decided you didn't deserve reality, or, to state it more exactly, have decided you were worthy of unreality, a kind of death giving. Now, if you would

pardon such murderers, what wouldn't you forgive
or by forgiving, allow?

Many Worlds

Grief, pain, loss propel us to our pluralized lives.
Few of us here are all here. That woman there
is always going down stairs to the basement
to meet a familiar child (herself) and her abuser
in a half light of heavy breathing and clanging
    pipes.
Another, on the T, a maid, stares at marble and
    mirrors,
the gleaming shapes of the restroom where she
    was raped.
The man selling you a car is playing ball with his
    brother,
the one who grew up and died in Vietnam while
    the man
who stood beside him on the firing line is obsessed
    with feet,
not the two he lost but mere measure ... six feet
    closer
he would have died, six feet distant he could walk
and so he limps along, his universe marked off in
    two yard spans.
In personal terms, these are cosmic catastrophes,
    Big Bangs

but worlds also multiply upon the action of moral atoms,
lies, each of which creates, at minimum, four dimensions:
the world before the lie, the world during the lie (strange physics!),
the planet Revelation where the air is clear but clouding
since just over the horizon, lies …
it's like the many worlds interpretation of quantum mechanics
except this really matters. No theory but your life or lives. Or lies.

168   Once you have acquired a hatred of someone, death becomes a friend because eventually, without your having to lift a finger, death will take care of him or her (or them).

169   Something can be said in favor of the tactically deployed inept sentence, the kind that falters in its drive to communicate, that stumbles and is even grammatically suspect. The reader draws up before it and if he or she is to continue, they must take the jump and press through the thicket. If the matter has any meaning, they retain it because they have earned it. To write in this way calls upon a peculiar finesse that good writers lack.

[That's good to know.] |cf.no.108|

An immense sum for one who daily asked his wife for money, his daily allotment. It was a dependency based, he fancied, more on her abiding needs than his financial inabilities – not that he was interested in money. Hers was the mind that required detail, liked things neat, tidy, and had for the decade of his marriage managed all accounts – and did the taxes. She was good at it, she said she enjoyed it. He remembered all those years in the small, Virginia college town, the span of her undergraduate and graduate studies, evenings when he sat by as she paid the bills, her hair two toned under the desk lamp, almost blonde in the circle of light, falling away in a dark flow that brushed the pile of canceled checks. He'd been happy then and believed she had been. But when the degree was finished (linguistics) and there was no job, she wanted to move. He delayed a year, pleaded projects at work, people he needed to train and watched as she went from forbearance to impatience, silence and despair. She was, he saw, disappearing, starving, self-consuming.

170 *War Horse*. At the end of the nineteenth century, it would have been possible for the nations of Europe to agree to an international covenant banning the use

of horses in either combat forces (cavalry, field artillery) or logistical transport. (Trucks and tanks were imminent.) Of course, if statesmen and generals were none too careful about the loss of men, why should they care about horses?[26] Yet everyone recognized that soldiers were enrolled, complicit in human values and activity, war being one of them. While many (not all) wives and mothers cried to see their husbands and sons go, the men marched off with pride or resignation. But when the horses were requisitioned, entire families broke down and wept. They knew the animals would suffer, weren't coming back and were utterly innocent. (And this grief not from loss as the farm's tractor since all nations allowed at least one horse to remain for plowing and other labor.)

171   "Men are devils on earth, and animals the tortured souls." – Schopenhauer.

172   It can be thought, screamed, voiced ten thousand times in every tonality in-between, the "why" that will never be answered – why you keep asking it.

---

26   However, Ruth Scurr, in her 7/13/18 TLS review of Michale Broers' *Napoleon* records that the master murderer of the nineteenth century was appalled by the routine British practice of shooting exhausted horses to prevent them falling into enemy hands.

173   But I would not have had that cup pass; bitterness too is a savor. |cf.no.27|

174   It's a thing the real estate agent can't tell you and that owners don't know to answer – how does this house sound in the rain? Some houses seem annoyed, others complain. Some seem cheerful, purposive. Most sound like nothing in particular, mere hydraulic gurgling. The best make a kind of abstract music. It's an important thing to know because if it is grief that prevents sleep, the brain can be beguiled listening to a house that's tuneful in the rain. |cf.no.45|

So, they moved, without jobs in hand (it was a bad market for linguistics). Despite his admiration of her, it had been a pinch of surprise to his ego when she was hired first. (After all, he had a track record as a library clerk). And at the great university, at the nationally known "Culture and Computers Project", a universal silicon-based lexicon of everything a cultured consumer needed to know. Just insert the disc and follow the prompts. Years in the making. She came home different now, later than he even though his job at the Catholic College of Newton involved an hour's commuter train ride. He learned to wait, cook his own supper, save some, if only notationally, for her and listen for the sound of her new heels on the outside steps then nearer and nearer down the hardwood hall.

175 *Family Circle*. Congenial, intelligent, rather sprucy looking in his high collar, bow tie and pin-striped shirt, my future father at age twenty-one works as a counter clerk at the general store, not a bad job for a young man in the small Virginia town, population three hundred. But he dreams of the big city (Newport News/ Hampton) and today is Jan. 1, 1901; the bright new century is all before him. Six decades later, he's sunk in a big brown recliner, not reading or smoking, just staring ahead, dying of cancer, thinking I'd guess, about his life, – how he had ended up in welfare housing with a fifty-year-old hapless wife and a six-year-old child. They are going to have to make do with his government warehouseman's pension. Something had gone wrong. If he knew what it was, he never said.

Not a drinker, gambler or womanizer, he wasn't a dramatic personality. He worked hard enough. Perhaps it wasn't a big thing that undermined him but a lot of little things that seemed hardly worth remedying, the way a few grains of sand can wear an engine down. An aspect of his last job, in fact, handing over small replacement parts – bolts, pins, flanges – to mechanics at Langley Air Force base. Midway into the century he had viewed with hope as providing scope for his ambition, he was still an on-call accessary behind a counter.

My mother, for all her good humor, was fundamentally a reactive type, patiently waiting for the next thing to get her twitching. From an early age, I saw my biological mission as not passing on my genetic heritage and in this, another of father's failures, I have been completely successful. (A triumph of the Will and prophylactic technologies: 3600 plus fucks and (as yet) no offspring. My positive assignment was to fuck with language. It was no recognized union but I hoped my bastards would thrive.) |cf.no.153|

176 *Virginia wine tasting:* This could be one of Dante's more agreeable lower circles, a place for punishing minor sins such as flattery and writing in library books by having to listen to tasteful lies ("P*ale gold in color, delicate orange blossom precedes aromas of ripe peach, apricots and orange zest. Deliciously opulent, the uplifting rush of apricot and peach are embedded in a rich mouthfeel that gradually fades into a tantalizingly long, one might say, "endless" finish."*) while drinking eternally replenished samples of unequivocal dreck. [27]

---

[27] "Nothing is worse than serving bad wine to dull guests." (Cheever) excepting, perhaps, serving pretentiously bad plonk to defenseless day-trippers. The pourer behind the bar was almost elderly but vitalized by her actress-like mastery of a small role. "Where do you come from?" "Here. Charlottesville." "Your first time?" I nodded. "What's wrong with you that you haven't been here before?" And wasn't she right in her assertive perception – as a local lush, wasn't this place, a waiting room for hell, a natural peregrination, more beguiling in its faux awfulness than any precinct of heaven I could believe in?

RR: Home Construction. By John Silver. At the center of this story that spans decade and continents is a single mother in Miami whose son wants her help in smuggling cigars from Trinidad-Tobago.

177   There are two types of illusions, those you recognize as illusions and those you don't. The second type is collectively called "reality."

178   Our lived "truth" is a complex mix of facts and falsehoods, fantasies and fictions. People, over-reactive to smallest lie, are oblivious to the hazards of excessive truth which, like pure oxygen, is liable to leave its recipients a mass of ash.

179   Intelligence easily fools itself or is seduced by clever deceptions; a good memory accentuates pain, conscientiousness can inhibit palliative adaptability. Intelligence, memory and dutifulness are not the absolute assets they seem but "modalities" (functions) whose value is subject to situations and circumstance. Sometimes it's advantageous to be dumb, forgetful, careless.

180   In our memories, we think of other persons as discreet identities who performed certain actions as a result of definite motivations. With the special insight of self-consciousness, we are more inclined to view ourselves and our own actions more ambiguously (and correctly) as expressions of largely unrecognized forces and drives. Our recollection of other persons, presented as "characters", is, to that extent, grossly inaccurate but enabling of literary fiction which "realistically" depicts our delusive inferences.

181   Rouchefoucauld writes "We always like those who admire us" and for once, exempting his dated characterizations of the sexes, he's dead wrong. Our estimation of our admirers is often laced with contempt. We know our flaws, some of them, and can hardly credit they (our admirers) can't do better than *that,* that is, us. (The decisive juncture: we are often vain but rarely self-admiring.)

(They'd been lucky to get a place within a mile of Institute, an old three decker, divided into apartments. While the building looked like nothing, a pale-yellow frame box with windows, the top floor was warm and bright and they hardly noticed the other tenants, lower on the stairs – two Chinese engineers and a couple that never came or exited together. "We're not like that." Susan had observed.)

She came home later than he. There was her quicker urban stride, the bounce of her cut, styled hair brushing full and nouveau riche upon the silk or linen shoulders of her new clothes. And the novelty of his almost regret at never having recorded her voice, for did he not detect a slight huskiness, a half hesitancy of display in her always cultivated voice? Their sex life, a language she called it, like Greek "with the structure to express whatever it wants" was unchanged in its success except for the hint of cologne she now brought to bed and the lacy things, the stockings and straps, as much gadgets to be mastered as the winking answering machine with its tiny cassettes spooling earnest messages, always for her. "Susan, Tom here. Call the shop. Thanks." What disturbed him was this – her laughter.

182   Hesitating to tell an acquaintance the truth: an indication that he (or she) is becoming a friend.

183   Friendship is never equal. Someone loves more and hopes that in time, the other party, by force of affection, will match the feeling. This balance is seldom achieved and that's a good thing since it

is inequality in the relationship, the differential of devotion, that gives it vitality and flow.

184 It is obviously possible to view the white margins between these paragraphs as *ma,* empty or negative space. But it is the textually articulative space that is truly negative. The energy of thought always converts into a matter/anti-matter pair. Any concept immediately generates its negative (Thus, "Charlottesville is in Virginia" is paired with the silent antibody "Charlottesville is *not* in Virginia.") As Hegel knew, all positive assertions are technically neutralized by their negatives, independent of truth value. It is the white space between propositions, a snow field of imminence, of the possible, that is the true positive. [Contrived.]

185 The experience of romantic, domestic, and contractual infidelities, however painful, isn't tragic. There is always a comic element (the stock, clueless cuckold of drama) to be appreciated (even by the victim) – one has been foolish enough to trust and equally, someone has been venal or venereal general enough to betray. Real tragedy lacks a pat formula though its instances are definite enough: a murdered child, the young getting the diagnosis of death, an animal that cannot comprehend its suffering.

186   Evil (of the non-violent type) usually starts out with a smile which, with time, becomes a scowl. That this is already known explains the charm of the smile.

187   His modesty, which insured he had no interest in currying favor with anyone, slowly metastasized into an indifference which didn't care what anybody thought about anything.

188   Some who desire the satisfactions of struggle are too reticent or timid to confront other people. Instead, they challenge themselves in an ever intensifying cycle of self-degradation and rehabilitation. Such self-destructive types generally end up badly but not always. Sometimes, in the positive phrase, they pitch themselves to such a point of success even they can't retreat from it. Certain actors and writers come readily to mind. It looks like their demons have finally been conquered when they've simply been materially overwhelmed.

RR: Rising Water. By Maggie Pye. An incisive novel about an elderly woman who tries to outrun death by being in constant motion, bugging her friends, spending days at the mall and touring historic gardens.

---

189   Feeling we are self-possessors of our lives, we naturally grasp what appears in them – the world in its immensity and variety. We make history like we are owners when we'd be acting more accurately and circumspectly as renters. For we own nothing, not our lands, houses, families, skills; everything is causal, contingent, dependent, temporary. Yet even as renters we'd want to be caretakers of the future and rightly so because if not us, who? The problem is our limited capacity. Curators of the future are usually careless of the present.

190   One of those ecstatic equivocations, like being on the verge of a sneeze but not sneezing or at the point of climax but not coming, being in the grip of fate but, as one supposes, not yet "fated."

There were people, she made clear, men and women at work she admired, men mostly, natural given the occupational demographic, the usual he gathered hard driving jokesters or wry guys, for all their mild style of hush puppies, academic tweed or, in season, corduroys. She came home with stories from her day and with a toss of her head, repeat some office joke and laugh fully, unreflectively, pleasurably as if at the first telling. He had never seen this before in her, an incandescent quality of delight in another; it had nothing to do with him. (He thought then of her precipitous and prolonged climaxes, surges that he only surfed and that also had nothing to do with him as a person). After the third or fourth such revelation, he understood he was seeing her as other men did, a beautiful, fit woman with the inviting maturity and elegant edginess that came from being no longer entirely young.

191   In the future, humans will be able to choose their sex from a smorgasbord of options including male/female genital duality. They will spend a lot of time fucking (Bosch's *Garden of Earthly Delights*, realized) in the new combinations because computers and robots will be doing all the work. A sentimental group will look back on our era of sexual simplicity "romantically", the way we view aspects, transportation (Horses! Carriages!), say, of Jane Austen's Regency.

A Garden of Delights

Hand on cheek, pondering,
you made your choice
and left the feminine lake,
your hair wet and clinging.
I vaulted from the cavalcade of males
to run where we could meet

and pretend to be sexual innocents
or take on the usual kinky roles:
me, the armored man, you a slippery undine.
Post-coitally blissed, we retreated to our private bubble
until beckoned out by bird calls and songs
we joined the naked throng swirling in erotic arrangements,
quintets, sextets, gay, straight, blacks, whites ...
you name it. Nature is promiscuous.
Must we pay for our pleasure?
Some say there's a crowded acoustic hell —
disco beats as the city burns, ears bleed,
all exits are blocked; a bad night of clubbing.
But it's nowhere near. We picnic in orchards, pick apples, play.
No cloud or shadow darkens this long summer day.

Lust

Bosch's "Seven Deadlies",
a pie chart of sin.
Let's examine everyone's favorite slice —
Luxuria, (Lust) the spice of life.
_____

Two couples are taking it easy in a stylish tent.
One gentleman lounges, a lady serves him wine.
At the back, a fancy dresser tickles a chin;

the women, practitioners probably of the oldest
   profession,
or update it if you like to the era of early Updike —
four swingers just after the switch.
Frankly, nothing much is happening.
The action's out front on the campground pitch.
Two fools are enraged and fight with sticks.
They seem out of place, strays, maybe from "*Ira*".
Then suddenly you get it, the moral clicks in —
Lust at its most intense is desire not indulgence.
The biggest sticks in the world won't get those
   clowns
pass the tent flaps of joy. Eternal exclusion.
You know the feeling. Each of us has stood outside
some pleasure pavilion and couldn't get in.
No satisfaction. Call it a sin.

(This set of poems, anonymously nominated, was awarded the 2014 Digby Dogbolt (Digby Cabot Dogbolt, American poet, 1916-1967) Prize for Poetry, administered by the Mendacious Foundation and Harvard University.)

192 At some time in the twentieth century, we reached the irresistible inertia point in terms of regulation and tampering with nature, with no going back except via catastrophe and only going forward towards ever more effective regimes of regulation

and control until somebody screws up, catastrophically, the controls. I remain an optimistic; clumps of people will always be planning their next fire, meal, move.

[If this is a Mayan cycles type model of social boom and bust, just say so.]

193   Amid the flux and fluidity of human emotions is the decisive determination of realizing you no longer love a certain person, place, thing. Like reading in the sunlight, the message is clear but glaring.

194   He was a rat in a maze. He'd have to choose many times between paths branching to the left or right with no standing still or going back. Eventually, he'd reach one of two exits, the cat or the trap.

195   Consider the many places you have lived. What is left of you in the rooms where you laughed and loved? Dust.

196   Most writers drink a lot. Painters get by, sniffing pigments and turpentine, imbibing the odd bottle of wine. Theirs is a much happier, healthier life. I've practiced both arts. As an artist, I think I'll make it to

age 82 or so. As a writer, I died ten years ago, twenty if I'd taken it seriously.

197 In every city, two types reliably appear fresh and well-rested, the innocent and the treacherous.

(Most people, bearing their freight of common guilt, look tired.)

198 The bleeding hearts are right when they say the transgressor we punish isn't, because of transforming time, the one who committed the crime. A fine doctrine until it comes down to me violating you. (I write as a confessed criminal. See no. 86.)

199 Let's not exaggerate the destructive aspects of self-degradation. Something is despoiled but it isn't you. You are always at the head of the parade leading a mob of your betters.

200 It is interesting to watch the welcoming ceremonies for foreign leaders. No matter how well trained the native band (the Germans, British, Americans, and Chinese are all excellent musicians), it never plays the alien anthem as well as its own. Everyone gets the message: there's no place like home – and negotiates accordingly.

201 The crux of the Kennedy assassination: not that the mafia, the oil boys, the Cubans, the CIA, the KGB, the KKK, the John Birchers did the shooting *but that they wanted to*. On Nov. 22th, hundreds were sighing in satisfaction – and frustration that they'd missed their chance. Presidents learned the lesson. Along with better protection, vetted crowds, an up-armored limo, the best defense was to lessen the assassin demographic by not making enemies. No attacks on invested interests or the deep state. (Trump, of course, loves to make enemies but he has never had the intelligence to imagine his own death.)

Framed

A child, I cried when JFK was killed,
when our charming, shining knight
was cut down by the shabby assassin.
Now I see that grief as a period thing,
a headline coeval with certain hats, hemlines,
   cars with fins.
Now we know: pro and anti-Castro Cubans,
Texas oil men, reptilian mafiosos,
the CIA, the KKK, cold-cocked husbands,
all were gunning for him that day
and have told us why, with what good reasons.
So many shots, so many Mannlicher-Carcanos ...
bathetic as a ballad, Kennedy's head explodes,

at the center of every plot, Zapruder's rose.
All dated, all fades.
What stays forceful and strange
is the ever-spooling reel of doubt,
a pale man between heavy deputies;
a reporter pushed his question, a microphone's barrel –
"Did you shoot the president?" Oswald's words rerun –
"I'm the patsy, I'm the patsy."

202   Easy to posit a definite date after which my life has simply been continuance. What was this date? Of course, it's of interest to no one but myself excepting the fact that almost everyone after age sixty has such a date, one generally more significant than that of their deaths.

RBC	5.45	4.60 - 6.20	M/uL	Final
Hemoglobin	15.6	14.0 - 18.0	g/dL	Final
Hematocrit	47.0	40.0 - 52.0	%	Final
MCV	86.2	83.0 - 95.0	fL	Final
MCH	28.6	28.0 - 32.0	pg	Final
MCHC	33.2	32.0 - 36.0	g/dL	Final
RDW	13.2	11.0 - 14.0	%	Final
Platelets	208	150 - 450	k/uL	Final
MPV	10.8	9.0 - 12.0	fL	Final
Nucleated RBC Percent	0.0		%	Final
Nucleated RBC Abs	0.00		k/uL	Fina

203 People lack the ability for self-criticism, specifically, the ability to question their basic beliefs. Here a test: write down five things you deeply believe about your life such as "my mate loves me, my work is useful, my children are happy." Then likewise list five about America; "the nation has reliable allies, representative government is the best kind", etc. In each set, the total truth value of your accounts is only 50%; some items are absolutely, others partially, false. If you say "I don't agree", my reply is, as above, you can't face the erosive truths.

204 I suspect every person has a certain key signature, a definitive tone of fundamental feeling (not quite the same as temperament, which is a less visceral emotional average), the most intimate thing about them; in my case, a sense of the machine rough running, of grit in the gears, of fatigue, the light of living being too bright. I've often supposed it was a specific illness – diabetes, low thyroid or clinical anxiety but no doctor thinks so. At all times distracted, I've missed a lot I should have been aware of, to my cost. Ostridge-like, I've wanted to bury my head in sand, which is stupid. Yet I give myself credit for knowing it was the head that was important. Maybe the rest would follow.

(John Cheever, in his journals, is very good on this effort to define one's key signature, to set the pitch to make the harmonies, especially in wrestling sexuality's dark and light into some resolution, his music a *lush* angst that can transpose even small squalors, such as discarded underwear, into a higher register. Mine? A standard march, not slow or quick, of one of the old, disbanded regiments, variations on an English folk song regularized and sharpened into 4/4 time that's, by turns, happy and sad and – like a man whistling down a dark road – too jaunty to sound the depths but acknowledging their presence.)

[Warning: contains Wine Writing. See no.33 for symptoms and antidote.]

205   One's sense of being alive, is it expressible? Art in this case a like good copy; it displays the flaws of the original very well but obscures its virtues.[28]

It occurred to him, as it hadn't since their early days of dating, she could be unfaithful. The antidote to his new, acute anxiety came to him immediately. He would betray before she did. He liked the idea. It was insurance against her freedom and any future injury. Looked at one way – the way he did – this was self-sacrifice on his part. True, it would cost money, which is where the lottery ticket came in. It was, in its bright

---

28   Cf. Rochfoucault.5.133

aluminum colors, a decoration he wore (inside his shirt pocket) the commemoration of his higher fidelity and, given the trouble he'd have to go through, traffic with prostitutes or escort service, the outward sign of his courage. He felt, as he not in years, superior to Susan in initiative and purpose and to all the tired people in the streets or crowded on the groaning trains ...

206   It's astonishing to discover that a mind as acute and generally congenial as Emerson's harbors not only incomprehension of Jane Austen but near contempt. Part of the problem is his being close enough to her in cultural sensibility not to be able to see the general contour of her particular virtues. This is always an issue, so ...we take a step back (or time takes it for us) and with the next step we can go longer make out the vital features. The perspective from which we can see most accurately and tolerantly is itself subject to very narrow tolerances so that intellectual scope and generosity, separately and together, are relative rarities.

207   Some scientist has just written another brilliant book about time. I have encountered at least thirty well regarded books on the subject that are worth taking time over. No one has exactly raised my objection, (though I've not read every word of the group) that

we are precluded from truth in the matter because our analytic tools, thoughts, are themselves sequential. Consider the greatest philosopher fish, very wise on the subject of water but he's never going to understand that what defines it is the utterly other – land.[29]

208   Again (see p. 7) studying KM's journals in my hit and miss manner, I read for the first time her account of the sick kitten. It's something you wish you'd never encountered but two seconds were enough to scan the words and now you know something that for the rest of your life you wish you didn't. You have to ask yourself, what kind of universe is this? Well, good, populated with healthy kittens and terrible with sick ones. That's all you need to know about the moral nature of things and broadly considered, all you ever will know. Oh – and that your life can take a turn for the worse with just two seconds of inattention – or attention for that matter. One second if a bullet is involved.

By way of Envoy It's past midnight and the snow has been falling for hours. It's quiet, no traffic and the plows not yet grating on the roads. The white night is luminous around the drawn curtains and the room is as bright as a summer's evening of full moon. I'm thinking about a book I just read – how reality is

---

[29]   The fish in question, whose school of followers is well established, was a Forehead Brooder.

made up of tiny particles moving at immense speed in empty space. We learn this in junior high school or earlier but it's another thing to think about it – how these same particles aggregated in nerve cells are the basis of our thoughts that conceive the particles spinning in space and of our perceptions of every object including the uncountable galaxies, the infinitely expanding universe. It all has a cat chasing its tail aspect; no wonder that in fascination and frustration, humanity has posited soul stuff to break the causal chain and resolve the mystery.[30] I never think about such profundities very long, moving nightly on to the women I have loved and desired. Meantime, my bedmate breathes easily and our cat snores on her corner of the bed as, unseen, the fine-grained snow deepens into tomorrow's white plain.

[Your last book was called *Vacating the Premises* (available from Amazon and fine book shops everywhere). Seems you didn't. May I suggest you call this one "*Rearranging the Furniture*"?]

(This book began with the usual authorial procedures aimed at production but after a while, I came to value the process over the product. I had no desire to finish

---

30 "The world of the subatomic meets the world of the inconceivably vast in quantum mechanics, which the human mind can understand only mathematically." (*Self and Mind*, S. Greenfield). This is astounding because mathematical objects and relations are real, *non-material* entities.

it.[31] If, as an independent reader, you have these words in hand, something dire may have occurred. See footnote no.3 for information and lexical directives.)

---

[31] Qualifying me, *per accidens*, for Nietzsche's accolade "I only want to read those whose thoughts became a book inadvertently."

Small Aphoristic Appendix

He figured he was about third best in the world at what he did but it was an activity (fabricating aphorisms) in which resided no more honor in being third than in being, say, 539th. It was a real temptation for him to think he was first (which was obscurely acclaimable) but he knew he wasn't and so, for integrity's sake, he rated himself 539th – and was arrogant about it.

The truth value of philosophical systems is, as Schopenhauer, Nietzsche and Wittgenstein knew, best expressed via aphoristic beta-decay.

Nietzsche was right to make aphorisms but wrong to make so many of them. You might think that was an easy mistake to make but you'd be too easily thinking mistakenly to think so. It was a lot work, as the best kind of error always is.

Funny: the myriad of minor aphorists (or moralizers) who write things like "Don't think, BE.' Or "The only time is NOW." Or "Today is the day you're waiting for." Odd they don't see or care that in writing down their dicta, they invoke and depend upon the world of language and literature which is never simply "here" and "now."

While I accede to the critique that these aphorisms are "all over the map", more accurately, they are the map, drawn from my experience of the world. Crude cartography of a small planet, perhaps, but adequate for the seasoned or armchair traveler.

Aphorisms are the perfect genre for the person who stays awake for hours, listening to his or her bedmate breathing in the perfect and imperturbable sleep of the guilty.

Generally speaking, do not compose aphorism about aphorisms.

[Because it is too close to self-parody?]

I found the aphorism a congenial verbal form for my creative efforts because it is an error free one. Aphorisms may be of variant power and effectiveness but there is no bad aphorism. If I write "squirrels love their oaks" and the overvalued word "love" implies some enhanced meaning to be interpreted aphoristically, it fails to reach aphoristic orbit and is self-relegated to a simple statement of fact. Weak aphorisms stifle themselves, they are still born. Working in this medium, I eschew doing the damage that was within my power. I did not write two bad novels, six books of indifferent verse and one book of futile essays. Just as my never owning a car or using domestic air conditioning was a positive environmental activity, so my literary negation I consider a significant artistic achievement, not augmenting the universal aesthetic degradation. "In art, it is often better to do nothing that something." – St Ludwig of Wittgenstein.[32]

(N's final verdict (No Appeal) on his literary effort was that even in a dim age, the occasional flares of his verbal intelligence did not compensate for the long no glow of no talent. Out, out, brief cant/dole.)

[You had to ruin even that, your epitaph. Ha-ha, hee-hee, I felt the thud of an English pun.]

---

32   [This is disingenuous. Nelson wrote four chapbooks of poetry: *Apex* (1998), *Gallery Effects* (1999), *Case Studies* (2000) and *Stern Ornaments* (2002), all published (and issued) by the Hetaira Press in editions of one hundred copies. He subsequently wrote seven books of "literary-mixed media": *A Wilderness of Monkeys* (2012), *Trooping the Colour* (2013), *A Book of Emblems, a novel* (2014), *Branches on a Wire* (2015), *Laminations* (2016), *Vacating the Premises* (2017) and *Frags* (2018), published and issued by Another Sparrow Press in editions of twenty-five copies, with at least thirty additional copies (among the various titles) printed as "on-demand items" by Amazon to satisfy the opportunistic appetites of a voracious readership. Bibliographers may find interest in sorting out various "revised editions" and "second printings" and in tracking down a lost chapbook, *Night* (1980?), an early edition of *Apex* (1986?) and two pamphlets: *Some Suggestions for Protection of Books and Manuscripts in a Home Library* (Alderman Library Press, University of Virginia) and *Save the Mounted Unit of the Boston Police Department!* In documents on file with the Internal Revenue Service (U.S.), Nelson is listed as "sole owner and chief executive officer of the Hetaira and Another Sparrow presses." Lector si monumentum requiris circumspice.]

Pseudocolophon

"It is a great art in the writer to improve from day to day just that soil and fertility which he has, to harvest that which his life yields, whatever it may be, not to be straining as to reach apples and oranges when his natural crop is ground-nuts. He should be digging, not soaring." Henry David Thoreau, journal entry of November 9, 1858.

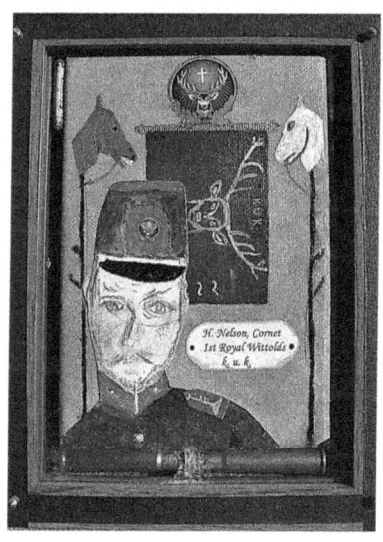

Page Nelson is the author of four chapbooks of poetry and seven volumes of "literary mixed-media" that comprise verse, aphorisms, critical essays, and fiction. His poetry and critical essays have appeared in numerous journals, on-line and in print. He won the Digby Dogbolt Prize for Poetry in 2009 and was a 2011 MacIntyre-McArthur Fellow at the Stevens House (Hartford, Conn.) In 2010, he was appointed Proctor In Aesthetics at New Courier College (New Courier, Massachusetts), a position he held concurrently with that of Technical and Reference Librarian at Harvard's Graduate School of Design until his retirement from both institutions in 2013. He now resides in his hometown of Charlottesville Va. with his wife, Laurie Kim (M.D.) and their five cats:

Ying, Yang, Sylvia, Scoop, and Nietzsche. Harvard's Employee of the Year (2013), he elected to receive the university's experimental "longevity vaccine" (Tiresiasimoan) as part of its beta-testing regime and is expected to live at least until 2038.

[An exhibition of his miniature paintings, including "Self Portrait, Österreichisches" (above, 4 x 5 inches, oil on canvas with Mauser shell casings), was held at Gallery 625 in Cambridge Massachusetts, Feb. 2013.]

In the bleak midwinter, frosty wind made moan,

Earth stood hard as iron, water like a stone;

Snow had fallen, snow on snow, snow on snow,

In the bleak midwinter, long ago.

Christiana Rossetti, in the musical setting by Holst.

www.ingramcontent.com/pod-product-compliance
Lightning Source LLC
Chambersburg PA
CBHW032136040426
42449CB00005B/274